A BRIGHTER FUTURE FOR MALDIVES POWERED BY RENEWABLES

ROAD MAP FOR THE ENERGY SECTOR 2020–2030

NOVEMBER 2020

ADB

ASIAN DEVELOPMENT BANK

© 2020 Asian Development Bank
6 ADB Avenue, Mandaluyong City, 1550 Metro Manila, Philippines
Tel +63 2 8632 4444; Fax +63 2 8636 2444
www.adb.org

Some rights reserved. Published in 2020.

ISBN 978-92-9262-513-9 (print); 978-92-9262-514-6 (electronic); 978-92-9262-515-3 (ebook)
Publication Stock No. TCS200355-2
DOI: http://dx.doi.org/10.22617/TCS200355-2

The views expressed in this publication are those of the authors and do not necessarily reflect the views and policies of the Asian Development Bank (ADB) or its Board of Governors or the governments they represent.

ADB does not guarantee the accuracy of the data included in this publication and accepts no responsibility for any consequence of their use. The mention of specific companies or products of manufacturers does not imply that they are endorsed or recommended by ADB in preference to others of a similar nature that are not mentioned.

By making any designation of or reference to a particular territory or geographic area, or by using the term "country" in this document, ADB does not intend to make any judgments as to the legal or other status of any territory or area.

Please contact pubsmarketing@adb.org if you have questions or comments with respect to content, or if you wish to obtain copyright permission for your intended use that does not fall within these terms, or for permission to use the ADB logo.

Corrigenda to ADB publications may be found at http://www.adb.org/publications/corrigenda.

Note:
In this publication, "$" refers to United States dollars.

Cover design by Mike Cortes.

Printed on recycled paper

CONTENTS

TABLES AND FIGURES

TABLES

FIGURES

FOREWORD BY HIS EXCELLENCY
HUSSAIN RASHEED HASSAN,
MINISTER OF ENVIRONMENT

Maldives' energy sector is firmly transitioning to an environmentally friendly sector by adopting renewable energy. Investing in renewable energy is a key priority of the Government of Maldives to minimize our heavy dependence on imported fossil fuel and to improve energy security of the country, thereby building up the country's economic resilience. Investments in renewable energy and energy efficiency give us the opportunity to lower our greenhouse gas emissions and electricity production costs and reduce the imports of diesel fuel, consequently reducing the burden on government finances.

Maldives needs to integrate renewable energy into power systems in all inhabited islands and resort islands, and to decarbonize the transport sector and industrial activities at a faster pace. The success of flagship projects such as Preparing Outer Islands for Sustainable Energy Development (POISED) project and the efforts of our utility companies have brought us closer to achieving our vision for the energy sector: "the provision of sufficient, reliable, sustainable, secure and affordable energy to citizens and businesses." The solar-photovoltaic-battery diesel hybrid energy systems introduced by the POISED project has been achieving fuel savings of up to 28% compared to diesel-only generator sets. It makes the case that investing in renewable energy is financially sound and contributes to de-risking financial investments in renewable energy in Maldives.

Transitioning into a low-carbon energy sector with decreased dependence on imported fossil fuels would, however, require addressing financial, infrastructural, technical, regulatory, and human resource challenges. This Road Map proposes two scenarios conducive to creating new opportunities for business, employment creation, and infrastructural developments. The base case scenario forecasts a continuous moderate transformation of the national energy matrix as we have been successfully achieving during the past 2 years. A radically more ambitious scenario is also presented in this Road Map. This paradigm shift scenario represents a fundamental transformational change the country aims at, and will have a profound impact on the national energy matrix and on the sector's business models. Walking the path of this more ambitious scenario will require the coordinated efforts of our institutions with international donor and development partners. The aim of this Road Map is to provide guidance to our government agencies, utility companies, and the private sector to improve their coordination efforts and alignment of external assistance to national policy priorities.

Hussain Rasheed Hassan, PhD
Minister of Environment
The Republic of Maldives

FOREWORD BY **KENICHI YOKOYAMA,** DIRECTOR GENERAL, SOUTH ASIA DEPARTMENT, ADB

ADB has been supporting Maldives since 1978. Cumulative loan and grant disbursements to Maldives amount to $402.29 million. These were financed by regular and concessional ordinary capital resources, the Asian Development Fund, and other special funds. ADB is committed to keep its support to Maldives in the most challenging times: On 25 June, ADB approved a $50 million budget support package for Maldives comprising a $25 million grant and a $25 million concessional loan to help the government effectively implement its coronavirus disease (COVID-19) response plan.

ADB will continue to support Maldives' energy transition. The revision of the Maldives Energy Road Map to consider the effects of the COVID-19 pandemic illustrates our long-term commitment to Maldives. Current ADB operations support efforts to enhance the country's energy efficiency, improve urban infrastructure and services, develop the private sector (including micro, small, and medium enterprises), and strengthen the capacities of the government in fiscal and project portfolio management.

In dealing with the high cost of electricity and the unreliability of power supply, the Government of Maldives and ADB have been working closely to replace inefficient diesel-based power generation grids with hybrid renewable systems through the Preparing Outer Islands for Sustainable Energy Development (POISED) project. This work is expected to benefit more than 160 islands, generate at least 21 megawatts of solar power, substantially cut carbon dioxide emissions, and reduce the subsidy burden on the government.

In addition to photovoltaic solar, many other renewable resources are still untapped. Marine floating solar, in-stream tidal conversion, ocean biomass, and wind resources can all be deployed with due consideration of environmental implications. Marine solar and wind are already cost-competitive with petroleum-based electricity generation and, in some locations, these are producing surplus energy, which is being converted to hydrogen and oxygen using electrolysis. Reef cultivation and sustainable seafood production can be colocated with marine energy production facilities with mutually beneficial ecosystem benefits, also interesting for the tourism industry. These energy resources can help diversify Maldives' economy and make sea transport cleaner, and the tourism sector more sustainable.

ADB hopes that this Road Map establishes guidelines for the energy transition, and contributes to economic growth, end of poverty, creation of employment, reduction of regional disparities in living standards, and resilience to weather severity and to other effects of climate change.

Kenichi Yokoyama
Director General
South Asia Department, ADB

ACKNOWLEDGMENTS

The technical study was prepared by a team led by Jaimes Kolantharaj, senior energy specialist, South Asia Energy Division (SAEN) and Sergio Ugarte (SQ Consult). The team is grateful for the valuable guidance and support of Kenichi Yokoyama, director general, South Asia Department; Yongping Zhai, chief, energy sector group; Priyantha Wijayatunga, director, SAEN; and Ronald Antonio Butiong, chief of Regional Cooperation and Integration Thematic Group, Sustainable Development and Climate Change Department. The team acknowledges contributions from Maria Charina Apolo Santos, project analyst; Karen Grace Ochavo, associate environment officer; and Marietta L. Marasigan, consultant.

The team highly appreciates the guidance of Hussain Rasheed Hassan, Minister of Environment, Maldives. It also appreciates the informative comments received from the Ministry of Finance; Ministry of Economic Development; Ministry of National Planning, Housing and Infrastructure; Ministry of Transport and Civil Aviation; Ministry of Fisheries, Marine Resources, and Agriculture; State Electric Company Ltd. (STELCO), and FENAKA. Lastly, it is worthwhile to acknowledge the support and inputs from the project management unit of the POISED project.

The technical study also incorporates learnings from the workshops on the Road Map for Low Carbon Development held in Maldives for capacity development of Maldives Energy Authority. The workshops were supported by experts in various aspects of renewable energy.

ABBREVIATIONS

ASPIRE	Accelerating Sustainable Private Investments in Renewable Energy
CO_2	carbon dioxide
GDP	gross domestic product
GHG	greenhouse gas
IPP	independent power producer
IWMC	Island Waste Management Center
LNG	liquefied natural gas
LPG	liquefied petroleum gas
NDC	Nationally Determined Contribution
NO_x	nitrogen oxide
OTEC	ocean thermal energy conversion
POISED	Preparing Outer Islands for Sustainable Energy Development
PPA	power purchase agreement
PV	photovoltaic
Rf	rufiyaa (currency of Maldives)
SAP	Strategic Action Plan
SDG	Sustainable Development Goal
SMEs	small and medium-sized enterprises
SO_x	sulfur oxide
SSLNG	small-scale liquefied natural gas
STELCO	State Electric Company Ltd.
SWAC	seawater air-conditioning
URA	Utility Regulatory Authority
V2G	vehicle-to-grid
WDC	Women Development Committee
WEC	wave energy converter
WTE	waste to energy

WEIGHTS AND MEASURES

kW	kilowatt
kWh	kilowatt-hour
kWp	kilowatt-peak
m^3	cubic meter
m/s	meter per second
MMTPA	million air-conditioning tons per annum
MTPA	metric ton per annum
MW	megawatt
MWh	megawatt-hour
MWp	megawatt-peak

EXECUTIVE SUMMARY

The Republic of Maldives comprises 1,192 small islands in the central Indian Ocean, with a population estimated at 533,941 people in 2019. Maldives has been a development success in the recent decades, mostly attributed to the revenues from a flourishing tourism industry that comprises around 25% of the national gross domestic product (GDP). The magnitude of the economic impacts caused by the coronavirus disease (COVID-19) pandemic has exposed the weaknesses of the economic model implemented in Maldives over the recent decades. It will take months or even years to reach the tourism goals of the country. The country's recovery will largely depend on the rapid transformation and diversification of its economic activities. Reliable and affordable energy supply are needed to address the transformation challenge. Maldives does not have reserves of fossil fuels, but it has abundant renewable energy resources, including solar, wind, and ocean. Investments in renewable energy are an opportunity to lower the costs of electricity production and reduce fuel imports and the burden on government finances. This Road Map establishes the guidelines to transit from a fossil-fuel-based energy sector to a cost-effective, business-competitive, affordable, and sustainable renewable energy.

1.   Road Map Ambition

Maldives' vision for the energy sector is the "provision of sufficient, reliable, sustainable, secure and affordable energy for a prosperous Maldives." This vision is sustained on three pillars: energy efficiency, renewable energy, and integration of technology innovation. This Road Map has been fully aligned with the country's Energy Policy and Strategy 2016 and the country's Strategic Action Plan (SAP) 2019–2023.

There are no proven reserves of fossil fuels in Maldives. However, it has abundant renewable energy resources, including solar, wind, and ocean, and the potential to produce green hydrogen fuel with the surplus of renewable energy produced in the islands. Maldives also has the possibility to substitute part of its diesel consumption with less expensive, more efficient, and less polluting small-scale liquefied natural gas (LNG).

Two scenarios conducive to achieve the country's vision are established in this Road Map:

- The base case scenario—achieving unconditional and conditional greenhouse gas (GHG) emission reduction targets as established in Maldives' Nationally Determined Contribution (NDC). This scenario forecasts a continuous and sustained moderate transformation of the energy matrix that will result in 29% of fossil fuels reduced compared to a business-as-usual situation.

- The paradigm shift scenario—representing a fundamental transformational change for the country beyond the target established in the current Maldives' NDC, with a profound impact on the energy matrix that will result in 52% of fossil fuels reduced compared to a business-as-usual situation. The paradigm shift scenario requires a strengthened policy framework and a well-functioning financial scheme duly considering the challenges and risks associated with the nationwide transformation.

Both scenarios were revised on May and June 2020 to preliminarily take into account the effects of the COVID-19 pandemic. The potential decline in energy demand of resorts in 2020 is balanced with the demand growth of industrial and agricultural islands. The Government of Maldives is actively supporting small- and medium-sized enterprises and farmers as part of its strategy for the country's economic recovery. As a direct effect of the pandemic, the zero-energy demand growth during 2020 is expected for sea and road transport, and more liquefied petroleum gas (LPG) would be used for cooking. For the period 2021–2030, more conservative energy demand growth rates are projected than those foreseen before the emergence of COVID-19. In absolute values, the consumption of fossil fuels (diesel, petrol, and LPG) is forecasted to grow from 674,000 tons in 2020 to 864,000 tons in 2030 in the base case scenario, and to 583,000 tons in the paradigm shift scenario (a net reduction of 13.5% compared to present consumption).

2.   Sector Assessment

Imported fossil fuels are the most important source of energy for Maldives. Fuel imports account for about 10% of Maldives' GDP. Approximately half of the fuel imports are used for electricity generation. Diesel is mostly used in electricity generation, industrial processes, and sea transport; petrol is mostly for road transport, LPG for cooking, and aviation fuel for airplanes.

Electricity Subsector

Maldives achieved universal access to electricity in 2008. Imported diesel, shipped in small quantities by boat to islands, results in one of the highest costs for power generation in South Asia. The most efficient power plants produced electricity from $0.23 to $0.33 per kilowatt-hour (kWh); while for many of the smaller inhabited islands, costs are as high as $0.70/kWh. Annual subsidies to the electricity sector amount to Rf1 billion ($65 million at the end of 2019).

A total of about 290 megawatt (MW) diesel generators is installed in 186 inhabited islands. Resort islands have an additional 144 MW in diesel generators and industrial islands about 20 MW. Power systems in small- and medium-sized islands typically comprise a few diesel generators, often installed with substantial reserve capacity that runs at very low loads during off-peak hours to cover for forced outages. A total of 21.5 MW of renewable energy systems are installed across the country.

The installation of rooftop solar PV panels in the Greater Male' Region has increased in the past 5 years, reaching more than 3,000 kilowatts peak (kWp) at the beginning of 2020. Hulhumale' sums 1.5 MW of rooftop solar PV operating since March 2018 under a power purchase agreement (PPA) contract at a fixed price of $0.21/kWh for 20 years. This infrastructure is supported by the Accelerating Sustainable Private Investments in Renewable Energy (ASPIRE) project, funded by the World Bank. A second project was tendered in 2019. The PPA is expected to be signed with the winner of this tender by the end of 2020. In this second project, a fixed price of $0.109/kWh for 15 years, with a capital cost buy down component, was offered by the project winner. In addition, 21,000 kWp are currently under pre-qualification, out of which 10,000 kWp are floating PV.

With an aim to transform the existing diesel-based energy systems of at least 160 islands into hybrid solar PV-diesel systems, Maldives established the Preparing Outer Islands for Sustainable Energy Development (POISED) project in 2014 with support of the Asian Development Bank (ADB). POISED is a flagship action that aims to install a minimum of 21 megawatts-peak (MWp) in PV installations. The concept design of hybrid systems (efficient diesel generators + solar PV + energy storage) has been a success for Maldives, resulting in an average fuel savings of 25%.

Buildings and households in Maldives account for a large share of the total energy end use. Most buildings suffer large energy losses. However, no statistics on their energy consumption have been recorded. The majority of residential buildings have been designed for the use of fans as the source for comfort air, though they later installed air-conditioners. Inefficient lighting and household appliances are additional factors for the low levels of energy efficiency in buildings.

Other Subsectors

All inhabited islands are connected by a basic nationwide transportation network of ferries and jetties. However, the price of diesel makes sea transport very expensive. The number of registered vessels increased to 50% between 2010 and 2018. However, there is no available information on the energy efficiency of these vessels.

Fuel consumption for land transport happens mostly in the Greater Male' Region. The number of registered vehicles has more than doubled in the period 2010–2018, with motorcycles accounting for 83% of all vehicles with an active registration in 2018. Same as with vessels, there is no available information on the year of manufacturing of registered vehicles, their efficiency, and the amount of carbon dioxide (CO_2) they emit.

Most of the LPG imported by the country is used in cooking. LPG is distributed in standard LPG bottles to the final consumer.

3.   Strategy for the Electricity Subsector

Flagship interventions are proposed around energy efficiency, such as investments on renewable energy and integration of technology innovation. Energy efficiency interventions aim to reduce energy consumption and energy costs, without lowering the quality of life. Investments in renewable energy infrastructure will focus on off-the-shelf solutions, including roof solar PV, waste-to-energy, and small rooftop wind turbines. Possible synergies with water desalination plants are also being considered. Technology innovation includes the introduction of floating PV platforms, ocean energy (tidal, wave, and ocean thermal), and energy storage using hydrogen and fuel cell technologies. The investment mechanisms chosen are PPAs for the larger infrastructure, and net-metering tariffing for small rooftop installations. Achieving the proposed targets is expected to reduce diesel use by 35% in the base case scenario and 59% in the paradigm shift scenario, when compared with a business-as-usual situation.

Greater Male' Region

The base case scenario for the Greater Male' Region estimates that by 2030, 10% of energy efficiency is achieved (compared to a business-as-usual situation). The paradigm shift scenario increases this target to 20%. Interventions in the supply side include:

- dual fuel choice (diesel – LNG) for the new generators planned for Hulhumale' (50 MW) and Thilafushi (150 MW) by 2023, provided that adequate feasibility studies are carried out to determine which small-scale LNG (SSLNG) options are suitable to Maldives, the space constraints at the power plants side, the economic impacts on STELCO, and the definite utilization of power produced by the future Thilafushi power plant;
- interconnection of the power grids: Hulhulmale'–Hulhule'–Male' (phase 1 in 2021) and Male'–Villingili–Gulhifalhu–Thilafushi (phase 2 in 2023); and
- reduction of distribution losses to 5% by 2030.

Energy efficiency interventions in the demand side will result in a reduction of the peak day demand from 206 MW to 185 MW in 2030 in the base case scenario, and to 164 MW in the paradigm shift scenario. These interventions include:

- revision and enforcement of building codes,
- implementation of a certification mechanism,
- implementation of a light-emitting diode (LED) street lighting program,
- implementation of energy efficiency labeling for electrical appliances, and
- phase-out selling of inefficient lighting bulbs.

The share of renewable energy in the electricity produced in 2030 is estimated at 13% in the base case scenario and at 38% in the paradigm shift scenario. Investments include the following:

Table E1: Renewable Energy Infrastructure for the Greater Male' Region
(megawatt)

Renewable Energy Infrastructure	Base Case	Paradigm Shift
Conventional renewable energy (PV over bridges, rooftop PV, onshore wind, micro rooftop wind, and waste-to-energy)	42.5	61.0
Innovative technologies (floating PV and ocean energy)	12.0	70.0
Total	**54.5**	**131.0**

PV = photovoltaic.
Source: Asian Development Bank.

Since the Road Map's ambition is to integrate more renewable energy into the grid and to gain energy independence, some degree of industrialization of the renewable energy sector, such as introducing PV testing and PV panel assembly lines, would be advantageous for Maldives. Testing facilities at national level for renewable energy devices would ensure technical standards are maintained. Local universities can also be included in the research projects done by various renewable energy companies. The integration of floating PV requires feasibility studies to establish the locations and technologies to be used, considering that lagoons are scarce in the Greater Male' Region.

Other inhabited islands

The base case scenario for the rest of inhabited islands estimates that, by 2030, 10% of energy efficiency is achieved (compared to a business-as-usual situation). The paradigm shift scenario increases this target to 15%. Interventions in the supply side include:

- interconnection of islands with submarine or aerial cable, where economically feasible;
- replacement of inefficient diesel generators with modern efficient ones; and
- upgrading of distribution grids to reduce distribution losses to 5% by 2030.

Energy efficiency interventions in the demand side will result in a reduction of the aggregated peak day demand from 116 MW to 105 MW in 2030 in the base case scenario, and to 98 MW in the paradigm shift scenario. These interventions include:

- efficient street and indoor lighting,
- program for replacing inefficient household appliances, and
- program for replacing the existing meters with smart meters.

The share of renewable energy in the electricity produced in 2030 is estimated at 39% in the base case scenario and at 48% in the paradigm shift scenario. Investments include:

Table E2: Renewable Energy Infrastructure for Other Inhabited Islands
(megawatt)

Renewable Energy Infrastructure	Base Case	Paradigm Shift
Conventional renewable energy (PV in hybrid plants, rooftop PV, micro rooftop wind, and waste-to-energy)	110.5	128.5
Innovative technologies (floating PV and ocean energy)	18.0	22.5
Total	**128.5**	**151.0**

PV = photovoltaic.
Source: Asian Development Bank.

Resorts, Industrial, and Agricultural Islands

The magnitude of the economic impacts caused by the COVID-19 pandemic has put Maldives' tourism industry at a standstill since March 2020. Economic recovery would largely depend on how fast the tourism recovers. The country's "one-island, one-resort" approach has been thought to mainstream social distancing measures throughout the tourism sector. It is hoped this approach can speed up the recovery of the sector despite all uncertainties.

Electricity consumption in resorts can be broken down into—40% for air-conditioning, 10% for refrigerators, 10% for desalination plants, 10% for lighting, and 20% for laundry services. This means that more than 60% of the energy consumption in resorts is due to energy use of appliances and buildings. Policies on appliances and labeling can significantly help save energy in resorts.

The successful implementation of these measures requires that Maldives explores and proposes incentives to resorts and a mechanism to monitor and verify the incentives claims. This Road Map proposes that the Government of Maldives establishes a "zero fossil fuel energy" label and program. The label of this program is to be used to actively promote sustainable tourism in associated resorts. Any financial incentive (such as duty exemptions) should be reserved only for associated resorts.

Fisheries, the second largest economic activity in the country, is also severely impacted by the coronavirus outbreak. In the recent years, fresh, chilled, and frozen tuna accounted for 70% of all domestic goods exports. These exports fell by 60% in March 2020 due to logistics difficulties in transporting shipments to Thailand and the closing down of boarders by the European Union, with subsequent stopping of all international flights traveling to and from Maldives. Some recovery has taken place since the European countries started to reopen their markets in mid-May 2020. Developing fish products with higher added value targeting premium markets is a possible recovery pathway; but making this happen will require policy attention. Maldives will also need to modernize and expand the capacity of Maldives Industrial Fisheries Company to increase its productivity and earnings. Additional financing under the POISED project will also consider the installation of ice-making factories powered with renewable energy.

Energy efficiency in all industrial islands is crucial for achieving the Road Map targets. In particular, energy efficiency actions toward large-scale cooling related to the fishing industry should be carefully designed. Fish and fisheries products require substantial cooling to ensure products are maintained at exceptional quality. These plans and actions should focus not only on cooling systems installed on islands, but also on those refrigeration systems installed on board fishing vessels. It is anticipated that more than 150 to 200 fishing vessels will be fitted with such systems by 2023. These investments aim to increase the resilience of fisheries activities carried out on inhabited islands. The government is also determined to explore the potential of aquaculture and reef fishing.

In relation to the agriculture sector, Maldives should increase production yields and variety by incorporating modern climate-smart practices that will require reliable energy supply. Farming in Maldives needs rapid transformation to reach targets of food imports substitution.

The base case scenario for resorts, industrial, and agricultural islands estimates that, by 2030, 10% of energy efficiency is achieved (compared to business-as-usual situation). The paradigm shift scenario increases this target to 20%. Energy efficiency interventions will result in a reduction of the aggregated peak day demand from 186 MW to 167 MW in 2030 in the base case scenario, and to 149 MW in the paradigm shift scenario. Interventions in energy efficiency include:

- energy audits and plans for continuous improvement,
- use of waste-heat recovery and renewable cooling, and
- efficient lighting and energy efficiency labeling in appliances.

The share of renewable energy in the electricity produced in 2030 is estimated at 15% in the base case scenario and at 50% in the paradigm shift scenario. Investments include:

Table E3: Renewable Energy Infrastructure for Resorts, Industrial, and Agricultural Islands
(megawatt)

Renewable Energy Infrastructure	Base Case	Paradigm Shift
PV installations	50.0	150.0
Floating PV with storage	16.0	50.0
Total	**66.0**	**200.0**

PV = photovoltaic.
Source: Asian Development Bank.

4. Strategy for Other Subsectors

Transport

The 2030 target for diesel consumption reduction in the **sea transport subsector** is 22% in the base case scenario and 42% in the paradigm shift scenario, compared to a business-as-usual situation. Specific measures proposed are:

- program for the replacement of old and inefficient vessels to improve the average specific consumption of vessels by 20% in the base case scenario and by 40% in the paradigm shift scenario;
- introduction of hybrid solar boats with a target of 2.5% share;
- feasibility study on using natural gas as alternative fuel for large vessels refueling in the future international cargo port in Gulhifalhu; and
- feasibility study and pilot project on the use of hydrogen-fueled jetties and on installing small mobile hydrogen stations on islands that can store hydrogen produced by excess renewable energy.

The 2030 target for diesel consumption reduction in the **road transport subsector** is 22% in the base case scenario and 52% in the paradigm shift scenario, compared to business as usual situation. Specific measures proposed are:

- program for the replacement of old and inefficient vehicles to improve the average specific consumption of vehicles and motorbikes by 20% in the base case scenario and by 40% in the paradigm shift scenario;
- electric buses, vehicles, and motorbikes with a target of 2.5% share;
- reduction of vehicle registrations and development of efficient public transportation; and
- feasibility study on using natural gas as alternative fuel for vehicles in the Greater Male' Region.

Use of Liquefied Petroleum Gas in Cooking

The 2030 target for the reduction of LPG use in cooking is 35% in the base case scenario and 50% in the paradigm shift scenario, compared to business-as-usual. This could be achieved by establishing an awareness campaign, promoting microcredit programs aiming at the replacement of conventional stoves with efficient and modern (electric) induction stoves, and reducing or removing subsidies to LPG used in cooking.

5.   Enabling the Transition

Going from a fossil-fuel-based energy sector to a brighter future powered by renewables is a capital-intensive commitment, especially for the islands. This has been a challenge due to the high public debt of the country and the economic reforms and socioeconomic barriers it must address. Maldives experiences many difficulties in structuring the financing of its development projects, including climate change mitigation projects such as those listed in this Road Map. The main limiting factor is the country's reduced public sector financing capacity. Sustained support by multilateral development banks, bilateral cooperation with donor countries, private sector participation, and in particular, alliances with foreign investors interested in the introduction of innovative renewable energy technologies are crucial toward achieving a low-carbon energy sector. Access to national financing mechanisms, such as Maldives Green Fund, Fund for Renewable Energy System Applications, Renewable Energy Development Fund, and Green Loan scheme are also needed for the successful implementation of many of the Road Map actions.

The financing required for the Road Map implementation is presented in the next table. Grants and loans, in addition to those already approved, amount to $490 million in the base case scenario and $715 million in the paradigm shift scenario.

Table E4: Additional Financing for Road Map Implementation
($ million)

Period	Base Case Scenario			Paradigm Shift Scenario		
	Grants and Loans	Private Sector	Total	Grants and Loans	Private Sector	Total
2020–2023	245	450	695	315	450	765
2024–2030	245	180	425	400	510	910
Total	**490**	**630**	**1,120**	**715**	**960**	**1,675**

Source: Asian Development Bank.

Lower generation cost from renewable energies would not only improve the financial performance of public utilities, but also reduce the need for budget support to the electricity sector, thus improving the country's fiscal sustainability. During the 2020–2030 period, the direct subsidies to electricity tariffs that could be avoided are estimated at $340 million for the base case scenario and $425 million for the paradigm shift scenario. These savings should be transformed into a financing instrument leveraging additional funds for renewable energy infrastructure, particularly for the most economically vulnerable inhabited islands. Furthermore, by reducing the logistical difficulty of shipping and storing fuel across a large number of islands, the cost of electricity produced with renewable energy would decrease.

The regulatory framework should constantly be revised to respond to new technical developments and economic challenges. The proposed regulatory measures are the following:

Electricity - Supply Side

- Continually revise the existing tariff and introduce new tariff structures
- Develop technical codes and standards
- Develop a "zero fossil fuel" program to channel incentives to private sector investments (i.e., preferential taxation)
- Introduce a targeted subsidy for electricity

Electricity - Demand Side

- Revise the building construction code and establish a certification scheme for buildings
- Develop energy labeling and a support mechanism to replace low-energy efficiency appliances
- Develop future regulation for a more collaborative engagement with consumers

Sea and Road Transport

- Develop regulation and technical standards to phase out vessels, vehicles, and motorbikes with high GHG emissions
- Establish a program to replace low-energy efficiency vessels, vehicles, and motorbikes
- Set up a cap on vehicles and motorbike registrations
- Promote sustainable public transportation and reduce the number of vehicles in the Greater Male' Region

Liquefied Petroleum Gas Use in Cooking

- Establish a program to replace stoves with electrical induction stoves

Institutional Arrangements

The most important institutional arrangements within the Ministry of Environment, the Utility Regulatory Authority, and energy utilities are as follows:

- **Ministry of Environment.** Prepare plans and conduct studies (i.e., national energy balance, national energy efficiency plan, and feasibility studies); monitor the Road Map results and conduct capacity building; reinforce the training and educational activities promoting gender equality and inclusiveness as already carried out under the POISED project. (This is crucial to withstand the threat exacerbated by the COVID-19 pandemic against the great progress achieved on this field by Maldives.)
- **Utility Regulatory Authority.** Verify the information submitted by utilities, mandate resorts to collect and submit information, enforce transparency from resorts and privately managed islands, and conduct capacity building for the Utility Regulatory Authority staff.
- **Energy utilities.** Explore in more detail interconnection possibilities, explore energy-water synergies, and conduct capacity building for the utilities staff.

6. Final Note

This Road Map has taken into account the medium-term effects of the COVID-19 pandemic on business and economic activities in Maldives. These considerations are based on government information and other databases available at the time of publishing this report.

1 INTRODUCTION

Maldives, with its 1,192 islands in the central Indian Ocean, is one of the world's most geographically dispersed countries. It has an estimated population of 533,941 in 2019.[1] Out of its 1,192 islands, 188 are permanently inhabited, 79 are leased for long-term development (mostly for agricultural and industrial purposes), and 293 are allocated for tourism development (145 operate as self-contained tourist resorts and marinas) (footnote 1).

The geographical peculiarity of the country makes it exceptionally vulnerable to climate change, weather severity, and external economic shocks. The development challenges of Maldives stem from these vulnerabilities. The most populated islands of Maldives are Male' (227,000 people)[2] and Addu City (35,000 people). The rest of inhabited islands are small islands with dispersed population; 27% of the inhabited islands have a population of less than 500 (footnote 2). The poverty headcount rate is 8.2%.[3] These characteristics make service delivery, job creation, and economic diversification very difficult.

Despite all these challenges, Maldives' development has become a success. The country has experienced robust economic growth coupled with considerable improvement of its infrastructure and connectivity. Consequently, energy demand has grown exponentially over the past 4 decades due to the extraordinary economic growth in tourism, fishery industry, sea transport, and construction. However, Maldives does not possess any domestic fossil fuel reserves. It depends almost entirely on imported liquid fossil fuels for electricity production, industrial uses, transport, and cooking. This situation imposes a significant fiscal burden on the government budget and makes it vulnerable to fuel price fluctuations. The Ministry of Environment is in charge of designing the national energy policy and planning and developing the energy sector. The Strategic Action Plan 2019–2023 establishes that, in 2021, the Utility Regulatory Authority (URA) for integrated utility services will be functional. This regulatory agency will have a mandate to revise electricity tariffs and set targets to utilities on losses and power quality indexes.

---

[1]   Ministry of National Planning and Infrastructure, National Bureau of Statistics. 2020. *Statistical Yearbook of Maldives 2020*. Male' City.
[2]   Population of Male' City includes inhabitants of Villingili and Hulhumale'.
[3]   World Bank Group. The World Bank in Maldives: Overview. https://www.worldbank.org/en/country/maldives/overview.

This Road Map establishes the guidelines for transitioning from a fossil-fuel-based sector to a cost-effective, business-competitive, affordable, and sustainable renewable energy. It has been formulated to serve Maldives' vision for the energy sector, and it is built upon the country's broader policy objectives: economic growth, end of poverty, creation of employment, reduction of regional disparities in living standards, and resilience to weather severity and effects of climate change. It aims to provide direction to policy makers, financing institutions, and other stakeholders, and help them effectively coordinate their efforts in creating an enabling environment for the needed investments.

Considerations Made in the Road Map due to COVID-19 Pandemic

The massive and unexpected economic shock caused by the coronavirus disease (COVID-19) pandemic has exposed the weaknesses of the economic model implemented in Maldives over the recent decades. Prior to the COVID-19 pandemic, tourism revenues had driven the impressive development of Maldives' economy. Compared to the same period in 2019, tourist arrivals in February 2020 fell by 11.1% and by 63.4% in March 2020. Large volumes of foreign direct investment and sizable external borrowings were frozen with the sudden halt of tourism. These direct investments and borrowings have been crucial for the country to embark on large-scale infrastructure projects. Economic growth in 2020 is projected to contract 20.5%. While tourism is expected to remain as the main source of revenue for Maldives, it will be a challenge to reach the revised tourism target of the country. The external borders of Maldives were closed from 27 March 2020 until 15 July 2020.[4]

The recovery of Maldives' economy largely depends on its capacity to become more resilient and reduce its dependence on tourism. Until 2019, 25% of the national GDP was from the tourism sector, followed by the construction industry at around 7%. In the previous years, the fishing industry contributed 3% to 5% of the GDP, employing around 20% of the workforce.

Strengthening the fishing industry and other primary sectors such as agriculture will reduce the expense on imports and improve food security. A rapid economic transformation will require the incorporation of modern climate-smart practices and technical precision. It should be based on the economic empowerment of small and medium-sized enterprises (SMEs) through entrepreneurship and innovation. A reliable, sustainable, and affordable energy supply for citizens and businesses across the country is key to achieving this transformation.

Investments in renewable energy are an opportunity to lower electricity production costs and reduce the imports of diesel fuel, consequently reducing the burden on government finances.

---

[4]   Government of Maldives, Ministry of Tourism. 2020. *Statement on Restarting Maldives Tourism.* 23 June (and further updates).

The Road Map has taken into account the effects of the COVID-19 pandemic with the following considerations:

- The potential decline in energy demand of resorts during 2020 is balanced with the demand growth in industrial and agricultural islands. The Government of Maldives is actively supporting the SMEs and the farmers as part of its strategy for economic recovery.
- Around 80% normalcy in tourism arrivals is expected by the end of 2022, provided that effective vaccination or treatment against COVID-19 is found in 2021. A humble growth of energy demand in resort islands is expected thereafter.
- Road Map scenarios also aim to facilitate the energy sector in fulfilling the government's intentions to increase agricultural production and explore the potential of aquaculture and reef fishing.
- There is no increase in the consumption of diesel and petrol by sea and road transport in 2020 compared to 2019, and lower consumption is projected from 2021 to 2030 compared to what was forecasted in pre-COVID-19 times.
- There is no increase in the consumption of LPG for cooking in 2020 compared to 2019, and lower consumption is projected from 2021 to 2030 compared to what was forecasted in pre-COVID-19 times.

2 ROAD MAP AMBITION

2.1 Sector Vision

Achieving a dignified life for all the Maldivians is the greatest priority of the government. Reversing the country's dependence on imported fuel and realizing a better future powered by renewables is possible for Maldives. With this aim, Maldives has defined the vision for its energy sector as the "provision of sufficient, reliable, sustainable, secure and affordable energy for a prosperous Maldives." This vision has three pillars: energy efficiency first, investments in renewable energy, and integration of technology innovation (Figure 1).

Figure 1: Vision of Maldives' Energy Sector

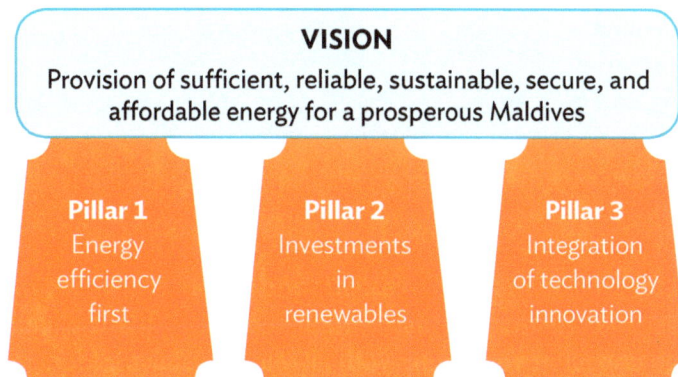

VISION
Provision of sufficient, reliable, sustainable, secure, and affordable energy for a prosperous Maldives

Pillar 1
Energy efficiency first

Pillar 2
Investments in renewables

Pillar 3
Integration of technology innovation

Source: Government of Maldives. *Energy Policy and Strategy 2016. Male'.*

Energy Efficiency First

Carrying out energy efficiency interventions to radically reduce energy intensity and consumption without compromising comfort and better living conditions is the first pillar of Maldives' vision.

Investments in Renewable Energy

Achieving a brighter future powered by renewables requires accelerating investments on cleaner and less expensive renewable energy sources. Renewable energy has entered a virtuous cycle of falling costs. Solar photovoltaic (PV) module prices have fallen by around 80% since the end of 2009, which will result in 50% to 75% reduction in the production cost of electricity in Maldives.

Integration of Technology Innovation

Identifying technology challenges and supporting the integration of evidence-based innovative technology solutions will help Maldives achieve more ambitious targets toward a low-carbon future. This Road Map adopts ADB's "3D approach" for a rapid rollout of cutting-edge technologies. This approach emphasizes piloting new technologies and sharing lessons with other countries (Figure 2).

Figure 2: ADB's 3D Approach to Addressing Energy Issues

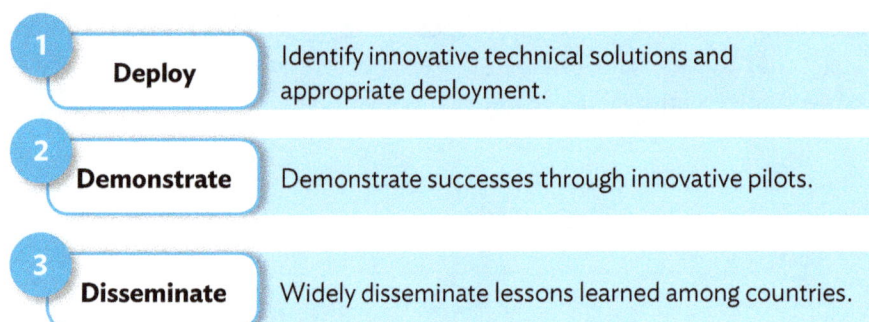

1	**Deploy**	Identify innovative technical solutions and appropriate deployment.
2	**Demonstrate**	Demonstrate successes through innovative pilots.
3	**Disseminate**	Widely disseminate lessons learned among countries.

Source: K. Nam. 2019. Financing the 2030 Energy Transition: ADB's Approach in Supporting Low Carbon Development. Presentation. Bangkok. 19 March.

Realizing the energy sector's vision requires a realistic and consensus-based road map that addresses multiple barriers—regulatory, infrastructural, technical, financial, and human resource barriers. After a thorough consultative process with all relevant stakeholders in the country, international and national experts, and other government agencies, the Ministry of Environment has developed this Road Map to open new development and business opportunities for the country, and facilitate the alignment of external assistance with the national policy. This Road Map will contribute to reducing dependency on fossil fuels and improve national accounts. The country will have the opportunity to capitalize on a low-carbon economy, create new jobs and skills, and cut energy bills. A low-carbon energy sector will, therefore, contribute to the economic growth of Maldives and the well-being of its population.

2.2   Renewable Energy Resources

Maldives does not have any proven reserves of fossil fuels. However, it has abundant renewable energy resources, including solar, wind, and ocean, and the possibility to produce green hydrogen fuel with the surplus of renewable energy produced in the islands.

Solar Energy

Solar PV energy is an indigenous resource with the most immediate exploitation possibilities in Maldives. Solar radiation is in the order of 1,200 kWh/m^2/year[5], which is considered good for any solar PV project. The solar PV project is being successfully implemented in hybrid systems in several inhabited islands through the Preparing Outer Islands for Sustainable Energy Development (POISED) project. PV panels are installed on the roofs of diesel power plants, schools, water desalination plants, sewage plants, and public buildings. PV panels are connected to the diesel power plants through an energy management system (EMS) that enhances the regulation of power supply. This hybrid configuration can offer short pay back times when compared to current prices of electricity produced by diesel generation sets. Rooftop solar PV is also being installed in the country, under net metering.

POISED = Preparing Outer Islands for Sustainable Energy Development Project. Solar photovoltaic panels on the roofs of schools and public buildings are connected to diesel power plants—forming hybrid systems (photo by Ministry of Environment).

---

[5]   ADB. 2014. *Toward a Carbon-Neutral Energy Sector: Maldives Energy Roadmap, 2014–2020.* Manila.

Floating solar PV platforms is a good alternative for some islands. These are platforms moored in the sea with mounted PV arrays on top. These PV floating platforms are connected to the island's grid using a submarine cable. These platforms must be placed in areas close to the islands and with low wave activity to ensure their operations withstand. Effects of salinity over the solar panels must also be considered in the design. Concentrated solar power is developing fast and foresees the incorporation of a solar stem that is also the storage medium (no battery storage is required). However, this technology could be constrained by land unavailability and economies of scale issues.

Wind Energy

Similar to rooftop solar, the urban small vertical axis rooftop wind turbines have the potential to operate in all inhabited islands under the same net-metering arrangement given to solar rooftop. These urban turbines are specifically designed to work under low windspeed conditions (2 to 6 meters per second [m/s]) found in an urban environment.

Conventional horizontal axis onshore wind turbines are also possible in Maldives, under certain conditions. Wind resources are not equally distributed across the country. The wind energy resource maps indicate that the northern half of the country is relatively richer in wind resource than its southern part.[6] Wind speed recorded at 40 meter height in 2016 showed an annual average of 5.69 m/s in Naifaru and 5.73 m/s in Gulhifalhu. Such wind speed is not as high as those for large wind farm projects in the world, but they can sufficiently compete against diesel-generated electricity. However, the economic viability of such projects needs to be further explored. Power grid capacity of each island, land availability, and logistics constraints have led to a scenario that only industrial islands in the Greater Male´ region have the potential for large-scale onshore wind projects using 2 MW turbines (estimated potential is 80 MW). For other islands, the deployment of midsize wind turbines of between around 100 kW and 300 kW rated capacity could be explored. Wind turbine noise impacts must be carefully examined for each case.

Offshore wind projects with current technologies are not economically feasible for Maldives. Seawaters in the Greater Male' Region (region with the largest power demand) are very deep and the atolls have very steep slopes. This is a huge challenge for the foundations of the turbines.

Ocean Energy

Ocean energy (from marine currents, wave, and thermal sources) is considered one of the most promising renewable energy resources for Maldives. Progressive development of ocean energy technologies and projects are key to the successful adoption of ocean energy for Maldives. Marine current, wave, and ocean thermal energy for electricity production and various co-applications such as cooling, desalination or water production, and initiatives toward a

---

[6]   National Renewable Energy Laboratory. 2003. *Wind Energy Resource Atlas of Sri Lanka and Maldives.* https://www.nrel.gov/docs/fy03osti/34518.pdf; M. Purcell and T. Gilbert 2015. *Wind Resource Mapping in Maldives: Mesoscale Wind Modeling Report.* Washington, DC: World Bank Group. http://documents.worldbank.org/curated/en/836871467997849102/Wind-resource-mapping-in-the-Maldives-mesoscale-wind-modeling-report.

green maritime ecosystem (i.e., green ports, electrification of vessels, smart bays and buoys) are particularly interesting. It is a major advantage over solar and wind energy that ocean energy provides a continuous stream of energy. This advantage reduces the need for any form of energy storage, which is usually expensive. This characteristic is particularly relevant for the resort islands where some of their services, such as laundry, air-conditioner, or desalination water plants, run day and night. However, their quantification is at the very early stages and most technologies are not fully commercial yet. A preliminary resource assessment of tidal and in-stream energy has quantified the potential in a range from 28 MW to 106 MW in selected channels and currents reaching up to 1.5 m/s to 2.6 m/s.[7] Current or in-stream energy is harvested by extraction technologies, such as marine current or tidal turbines, placed in the water where fast-flowing currents turn the turbine blades (similar to what wind does with wind turbines). Wave energy is also potentially an important source of renewable energy for Maldives. A constant stream of waves propagated from the South Pole and across the Indian Ocean reaches Maldives. Wave energy installations face a low risk of damage from extreme weather conditions as Maldives is not prone to hurricanes or typhoons. A recent study indicates good potential of 8.46 kW/m to 12.75 kW/m.[8] Ocean thermal energy conversion (OTEC) may also become promising in the future once OTEC technologies reach commercial stages of development.

■ **Okinawa Institute of Science and Technology Wave Energy Project.** Two wave energy converter units are being tested at the southeast side of Kandooma island (South Male-atoll) (photos by Ministry of Environment).

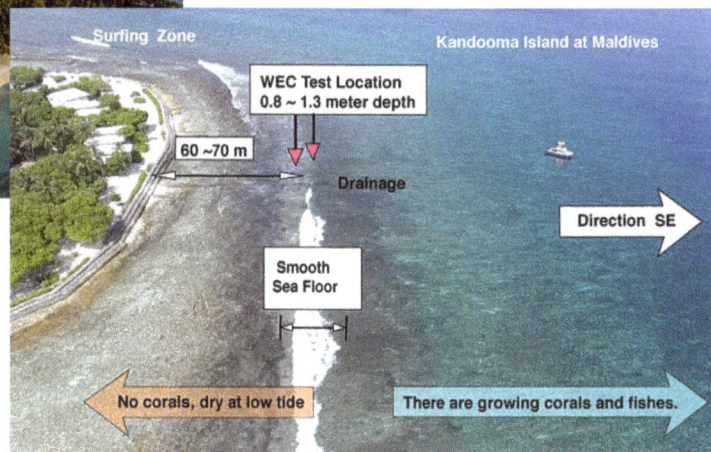

---

[7] Centre for Understanding Sustainable Practice, Robert Gordon University. 2011. *Marine Energy in Maldives: Pre-Feasibility Report on Scottish Support for Maldives Marine Energy Implementation.* Aberdeen

[8] P. Contestabile et al. 2017. Offshore Wind and Wave Energy Assessment around Male' and Magoodhoo Island, Maldives. *Sustainability.* 9 (4). p. 613. DOI: 10.3390/su9040613.

As the potential of these types of energy is affected by atoll configurations, more precise assessments are needed to initially find areas where resource and consumption exist in an aligned manner (i.e., not too far from each other that it becomes economically impractical). A memorandum of understanding (MOU) was signed in 2018 between the Ministry of Environment, the Okinawa Institute of Science and Technology Graduate University (OIST), and the Kokyo Tatemono Company Limited of Tokyo, to test until the end of 2020 two prototype wave energy converter (WEC) units 50 meters offshore along the shoreline of the southeast part of Kandooma resort island at South Male-atoll. The outcomes of the research so far are very promising and show a potential for commercial scale projects.

Biomass Energy

Biomass resources, mostly coconut shells and coconut oil, are also available, but constrained because they are distributed in much dispersed small quantities across the country. Those amounts are too small for local solutions, and their collection would be too complex and carbon-intensive to bring them to a place with large energy demand. Marine biomass may become an interesting resource in the long term when technologies for converting them into energy are cost-effective. No assessment on the potential of marine biomass exists at the moment.

Green Hydrogen Fuel

The surplus of renewable energy produced in the islands can be converted to hydrogen and oxygen using electrolysis. Hydrogen can be stored, transported, and used as fuel in internal combustion engines. This is an option for retrofitted ferries and jetties currently running on diesel. Reducing the cost of electrolysis or other separation methods is currently a critical challenge facing the commercial production of green hydrogen. Another key challenge in demonstrating feasibility is securing advance market commitments whereby energy consumers contract for long-term purchase of hydrogen. The business model for the production, storage, and transport of green hydrogen may follow some of the practices used for offshore oil and gas production and offshore wind power projects.

2.3   Possibilities for Liquefied Natural Gas

The global liquefied natural gas (LNG) market has become reasonably diversified in terms of suppliers, geographies, and countries. Compared to diesel, in general, the use of LNG improves efficiency in power generation, heating or cooling processes, and combustion engines. LNG has a strong track record of safety and reliability over the past 50 years, and instances of force majeure have been rare. LNG is also historically less expensive than diesel, though it has higher handling costs. The substitution of diesel with LNG represents an important opportunity for the Greater Male' Region due to the region's growing energy demand and corresponding increased pollution.

At present, it is possible to transport LNG at small scale by breaking bulk at conventional LNG import terminals or mid-sea LNG carriers and distributing it in smaller sized parcels directly to end users using a combination of sea and land transport (Figure 3). Small-scale LNG (SSLNG) can be built as modular structures with options to build upon existing infrastructures (e.g., harbors, jetty, and access roads).

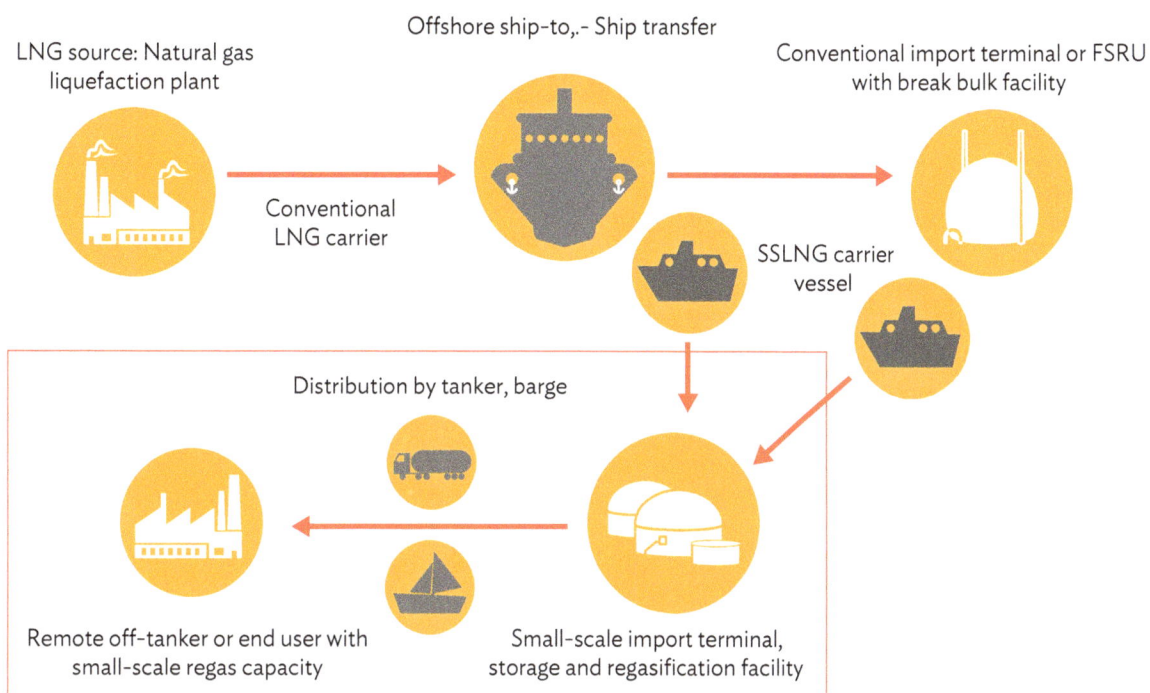

Figure 3: Alternatives for Liquefied Natural Gas Supply to the Greater Male' Region

FSRU = floating storage regasification unit, LNG = liquefied natural gas, SSLNG = small-scale liquefied natural gas.
Source: PricewaterhouseCoopers. 2017. Presentation at the High-Level Workshop on Preparing the Energy Road Map for Maldives. July.

The capacity of reception terminals can be increased at a later stage with a surge in demand. Small-scale LNG is in operation in countries like the People's Republic of China, Japan, Spain, Portugal, Norway, and other northern European countries. The costs for the LNG reception terminal are estimated between $50 million and $100 million. Table 1 presents an overall comparison between conventional size LNG and SSLNG reception terminals.

The global LNG market is reasonably diversified in terms of suppliers, geographies, and countries, and this diversity has been increasing rapidly in the recent past. The LNG market has had a strong track record of safety and reliability over the past 50 years and instances of force majeure have been rare. The transport of LNG in smaller cryogenic ships is nowadays economically feasible. Ships of various sizes are available ranging from 7,500 cubic meters (m³) to 220,000 m³ LNG. Possible LNG supply locations to Maldives are:[9]

- Kochi, India at 400 nautical miles distance;
- Colombo, Sri Lanka at 450 nautical miles distance;
- Dahej, India at 1,200 nautical miles distance; and
- Oman at 1,350 nautical miles distance.

[9]   ICF International Inc. 2018. *LNG Study for Power Generation in Male'*. New Delhi.

Table 1: Comparison of Conventional and Small-Scale Liquefied Natural Gas Infrastructure

Characteristic	Conventional LNG	Small-Scale LNG
Terminal size	5–10 MMTPA	100 MTPA-1 MMTPA
Capital cost	$1 billion to $1.5 billion	$50 million to $100 million
Trans-shipment medium	Large LNG cargos (30,000 m³–60,000 m³)	Small LNG cargos (1,000 m³–8,000 m³)
Gestation period	More than 5 years	~6 months
Liquefaction/regasification facility	Large liquefaction/regasification facility near import terminal	Small liquefaction/regasification unit mostly at customer premises

LNG = liquefied natural gas, m³= cubic meters, MTPA = metric tons per annum, MMTPA = million metric tons per annum
Source: ICF International Inc. 2018. *LNG Study for Power Generation in Male'*. New Delhi.

A specific feasibility study is needed to determine the best supply and infrastructure option. Three options are, in principle, possible for designing the reception of LNG for the new Thilafushi power plant:

(i)   Storage and regasification units located next to the power plant
(ii)   Floating storage and regasification barge (FSRB) anchored closed to the power plant
(iii)   Use of a container ship and International Organization for Standardization containers for LNG distribution to the power plant

LNG use in the Greater Male' Region would be, in particular, relevant for the following applications:

- **Power.** Large-scale production of electricity in LNG or dual fuel engines and turbines.
- **Industry.** Natural gas distributed through pipelines could substitute the fuel used in co-generation (power and heat), heating, and cooling processes.
- **Sea transport.** LNG and dual fuel engines are an increasing option for tankers, container vessels, and cruises. Vessels running on LNG achieve emissions savings of around 85% in nitrogen oxide (NO_x) as well as cut their sulfur oxide (SO_x) emissions by 99%. The installation of small-scale LNG infrastructure in the Greater Male' Region gives the opportunity to install an LNG filling station close to Male's main port.
- **Road transport.** Natural gas is in general less expensive than gasoline. Natural gas-fueled vehicles emit 20% to 29% less CO_2 than diesel and gasoline. Emissions of natural gas are cleaner, with lower emissions of carbon and lower particulate emissions per equivalent distance traveled. Another advantage of using natural gas is that it tends to corrode and wear the parts of an engine less rapidly than gasoline.

Outside the Greater Male' Region, LNG could represent a cost reduction opportunity for large resort islands that ship small amounts of LNG from Male' for a resort's semi-industrial processes and power production.

2.4   Policy Framework

Guiding Principles

For many years, policy making in Maldives has been supportive of the country's vision for the energy sector. Since early 2008, Maldives has called upon a cut in global greenhouse gas emissions, warning that rising sea levels could submerge the entire country. The Energy Action Plan 2009–2013 includes a series of energy efficiency interventions and conservation awareness aiming to reduce the country's CO_2 emissions. The 2010 National Energy Policy has pledged to carbon neutrality by 2020, and to provide all citizens with access to an affordable and reliable supply of electricity. The 2012 Maldives Scaling-Up Renewable Energy Investment Plan has put forward a strategy to scale-up renewable energy in the country. Maldives has also played a coherent and prominent role in international climate change discussions. Maldives' Nationally Determined Contribution (NDC) submitted to the United Nations Framework Convention on Climate Change (UNFCCC) has established the country's intention to reduce its greenhouse gas (GHG) emissions by 10% compared to business as usual by 2030 unconditionally, and by 24% under the condition of sufficient availability of financial resources and international support for technology transfer and capacity building. The type of Maldives' contribution through its NDC focuses on the reduction of GHG emissions in the energy, tourism, waste, water, and building sectors.

The policy instruments supporting Maldives' vision for its energy sector are the Energy Policy and Strategy 2016 and the Strategic Action Plan (SAP) 2019–2023. The Energy Policy and Strategy 2016 has established seven guiding principles (Figure 4). The SAP puts citizen engagement, inclusivity, and sustainability at the center of the national development model. The SAP identifies development priorities, steers national efforts, and outlines achievable targets for a 5-year period. Together, the Energy Policy and the SAP constitute the regulatory framework under which this Road Map has been elaborated. One of the five areas covered by the SAP is "Jazeera Dhiriulhun," which can be literally translated into "island life." The policy priorities and targets for "Jazeera Dhiriulhun" that are relevant for this Road Map are described in the next paragraphs.

Figure 4: Guiding Principles of Maldives' Energy Regulatory Framework

1 **Create** an enabling environment for the growth of a reliable and sustainable energy sector and meet the constitutional obligation of providing electricity to every inhabited island.

2 **Reduce** overreliance of the energy sector and the national economy on fossil fuels through the diversification of energy supplies.

3 **Improve** energy efficiency and energy conservation.

4 **Encourage** the adoption of low-carbon technologies in the production, distribution, and energy consumption through promotion of a healthy lifestyle.

5 **Exploit** local energy resources and renewable technologies.

6 **Engage** private sector participation in the development of the energy sector, energy services, and quality assurance mechanisms.

7 **Ensure** energy equity through social protection and mechanisms and/or safety nets for vulnerable groups of the population.

Source: Government of Maldives. *Energy Policy and Strategy 2016*. Male'.

Clean Energy

Energy demand in Maldives has grown exponentially over the past 4 decades due to the extraordinary economic growth in tourism, fishery industry, sea transport, and construction. Maldives does not have any proven domestic reserves of fossil fuels. Consequently, the country is excessively dependent on imported fuels and vulnerable to price fluctuations.

The government considers that it is crucial to invest on renewable energy to improve energy security and reverse the country's dependence on imported fossil fuels. Table 2 presents the SAP policies and targets for clean energy that are relevant for this Road Map.

Table 2: Relevant Strategic Action Plan Policies and Targets for Clean Energy

Policy	Targets by 2023
1. Ensure access to affordable and reliable supply of electricity to all citizens.	• Electricity subsidy should be implemented on a means-tested basis. • Reduce distribution inefficiency by maintaining distribution loss within 7%.
2. Expand and develop the renewable energy sector.	• Share of renewable energy in the national energy mix increased by 20% compared to 2018 levels (4%). • At least 10 MW of solar PV is installed under net-metering regulation.
3. Increase national energy security through diversification of sources for energy production and expansion of energy storage.	• Reduce fuel usage for electricity generation by 40 million liters. • Renewable energy storage capacity is increased to 30 MWh.
4. Strengthen the institutional and regulatory framework of the energy sector.	• Utility Regulatory Authority for integrated utility services functional by 2021. • New public infrastructure projects shall have provision to install renewable energy. • Energy data are up to date and reliable, and utilized for policymaking.
5. Promote energy conservation and efficiency.	• Green labeling is implemented for the energy sector. • Provisions for green procurement in the Public Finance Act is implemented by 2022.

MW = megawatt, MWh = megawatt-hour, PV = photovoltaic.
Source: Government of Maldives. *Strategic Action Plan (SAP) 2019–2023*. Male'.

Waste as a Resource

The most pressing environmental issue at present in Maldives is waste management. Open burning of waste is still widely practiced in several islands. Over the last 10 years, the Greater Male' Region has increased its waste generation by 155%, and the rest of atolls by 57.6%. Today, the country generates approximately 860 metric tons of solid waste per day.[10]

The fraction of organic waste is the largest stream, followed by the plastic and paper waste fractions. Most of the inhabited islands have Island Waste Management Centers (IWMCs), where waste is collected. Machinery and technical know-how are deficient in these facilities. Most of them lack the basic equipment required for effective waste management. In the case of the Greater Male' Region, the artificial island of Thilafushi was developed to collect and treat the Region's household waste.

The government recognizes that waste is a valuable resource and that it can be integrated in a cradle-to-grave approach following international waste management practices. Under this policy direction, single-use plastic is expected to be fully banned in Maldives by 2023.

---

[10] Government of Maldives, Ministry of Environment and Energy. 2016c. *State of the Environment Report*. Male'.

Pending in Maldives' waste policy agenda are the mechanisms to address hazardous, liquid, and electronic waste. In relation to the energy sector, Table 3 presents the SAP policy priorities and targets that are relevant for this Road Map.

Table 3: Relevant Strategic Action Plan Policy Priorities and Targets for Using Waste as Resource

Policy Priority	Target by 2023
Promote waste as a valuable resource for income generation.	At least 30% of Island Waste Management Centers (IWMCs) utilize solar energy for operation.

Source: Government of Maldives. *Strategic Action Plan (SAP) 2019–2023*. Male'.

Water and Sanitation

Freshwater comes only from rain-fed aquifers formed in Maldives. These aquifers are formed naturally at an average depth of 1 to 1.5 meters underground (footnote 10). Deterioration of groundwater quality is mainly due to saltwater intrusion, contamination from untreated waste, wastewater disposal, and mechanization of water extraction methods. Prolonged dry periods impose potential water security threats to the islands. The yield and quality of these aquifers is constantly affected by the sea level rise induced by climate change between 2012 and 2030—and yield is expected to decrease by more than 3%.

Maldives was pushed to modernize the country's sewage systems in the 1970s and 1980s, after several disease outbreaks had been linked to the consumption of water from contaminated aquifers. At present, 57% of the population has access to sewerage networks. Significant efforts are still needed to prevent the disposal of raw untreated sewage into the ocean (footnote 10).

Tap water provided by MWSC is safe for drinking in Greater Male' Region. However, approximately 76% of the total households in the Greater Male' Region prefers bottled water to tap water.[11] Ensuring safer and reliable drinking water, and modern sewage systems and treatment plants, require reliable energy supply. Table 4 presents the SAP policy priorities and targets for water and sanitation that are relevant for this Road Map.

Table 4: Relevant Strategic Action Plan Policy Priorities and Targets for Water and Sanitation

Policy Priority	Target by 2023
Adopt cost-effective and environment-friendly water and sewerage infrastructure.	• All inhabited islands will have access to safe water supply and sewerage facilities. • 30% of energy consumption for water and sewerage facilities across Maldives will be met with renewable energy.

Source: Government of Maldives. *Strategic Action Plan (SAP) 2019–2023*. Male'.

---

[11] Government of Maldives, Ministry of Health. 2019. *Maldives Demographic and Health Survey*. Male'.

Transport

Maldivian people are scattered across hundreds of small islands. This unique characteristic requires efficient and affordable transportation systems. An Integrated Transportation Network (ITN) has been established in Maldives to achieve inclusive growth. The transportation sector is essential and decisive for ensuring that basic items such as food, fuel, and medicine are provided across the country. Provision of inter-island transport is crucial for Maldives, as well the delivery and access to social services such as health care, higher education, and qualified employment. The large dispersion of people and high costs of fuel discourage investments by the private sector. The lack of investment in sea and air transportation takes a toll on social and economic growth, hindering sustainable development. In relation to road transport, the use of private vehicles is preferred over the use of public transportation in the Greater Male' Region. This causes an increase of fuel use and high levels of road congestion. Table 5 presents the SAP policy priorities and targets for transport that are relevant for this Road Map.

Table 5: Relevant Strategic Action Plan Policy Priorities and Targets for Transport

Policy Priority	Targets by 2023
1. Strengthen legal and regulatory framework of the maritime sector.	• Maritime trade is regulated through a legal and regulatory framework compliant to International Maritime Organization.
2. Strengthen maritime infrastructure and services to enhance socioeconomic growth.	• An efficient public ferry service is operational in all administrative islands.
3. Strengthen air transport and maintain a liberal aviation policy that benefits tourism and trade.	• 90% of the resident population have access to air connectivity within a 30-minute radius by speed boat.
4. Increase concerted efforts to reduce congestion and ease accessibility to roads in the Greater Male' Region.	• Vehicle congestion is reduced by 30% compared to 2018 levels. • At least 60% of the population regularly use sustainable public transportation.

Source: Government of Maldives. *Strategic Action Plan (SAP) 2019–2023*. Male'.

2.5 Scenarios

Two road map scenarios conducive to achieve Maldives' vision for the energy sector have been carefully designed for the interrelation of knowledge and learning, policy and institutional frameworks, and business models and finance (Figure 5). Both scenarios aim to achieve the SAP targets by 2023 and additional targets by 2030:

(i) Base case scenario aims to achieve unconditional and conditional GHG emission reduction targets as established in Maldives' Nationally Determined Contribution (NDC).

(ii) Paradigm shift scenario represents a large national effort for a truly ambitious target, beyond the target established in the current Maldives' NDC.

Figure 5: Interrelations Aimed at Enabling Environment

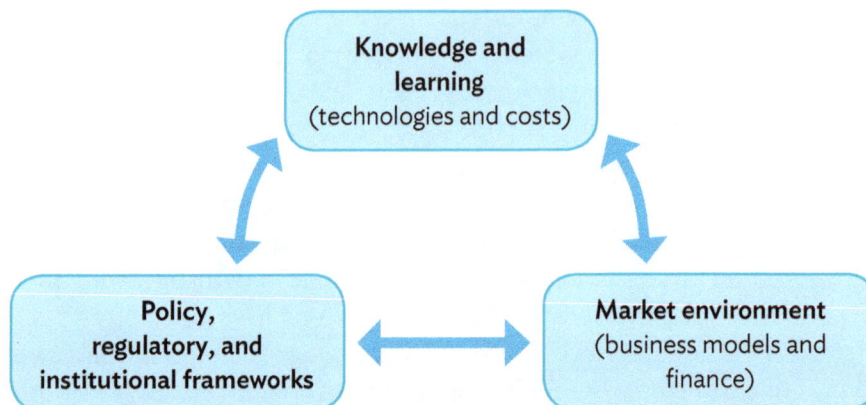

```
         ┌─────────────────────────┐
         │   Knowledge and          │
         │   learning               │
         │ (technologies and costs) │
         └─────────────────────────┘
           ↗                    ↖
          ↙                      ↘
┌──────────────────────┐  ┌──────────────────────┐
│ Policy,              │  │ Market environment   │
│ regulatory, and      │←→│ (business models and │
│ institutional        │  │ finance)             │
│ frameworks           │  │                      │
└──────────────────────┘  └──────────────────────┘
```

Source: Asian Development Bank.

These two road map scenarios build up on the priorities, targets, and strategies established by the Strategic Action Plan 2019–2023. They establish actions and targets independently for three subsectors: electricity, transport, and the liquefied petroleum gas (LPG) used in cooking. Table 6 specifies the general assumptions used in the three subsectors.

Table 6: General Assumptions Used in Road Map Scenarios

Electricity (diesel)	Transport (diesel and petrol)	Cooking (LPG)
• **Three differentiated geographic scopes:** Greater Male' Region, other inhabited islands, resorts, industrial, agricultural islands. • **Technologies:** Energy efficiency hybrid renewable energy-diesel plants, PV (rooftop, ground-mounted, and floating solar panels), small wind over roofs, waste-to-energy, and ocean energy. • **Storage:** Li-ion batteries in the short term; introduction of hydrogen storage after 2026.	• **Sea transport:** mostly dependent on diesel. Technologies: Efficient engines and solar boats; vessels fueled by LNG may also be an option. • **Road transport:** in the Greater Male' Region, and mostly petrol dependent. Technologies: Efficient engines, hybrid and electrical vehicles or bikes. • **Air transport excluded** from this Road Map.	• **Double use of fuels:** Cooking with LPG uses more than just the LPG since imported LPG is transported in bottles by ferry to islands • **Replacement technology:** LPG stoves replaced by electrical induction stoves; the possibility to use natural gas distributed by pipelines to consumers in Greater Male' Region should also be further studied.

LPG = liquefied petroleum gas, LNG = liquefied natural gas, PV = photovoltaic.
Source: Asian Development Bank.

Base Case Scenario

The base case scenario corresponds to achieving the SAP targets for 2023 and the unconditional and conditional targets established in Maldives' NDC for 2030. This scenario forecasts a continuous and sustained moderate transformation of the national energy matrix that will result in a reduction of fossil fuels to 29% compared to a business-as-usual situation. This scenario does not only impact electricity supply and fuels used in transportation and cooking. It also impacts the reliability and competitiveness of groundwater management and wastewater infrastructure. The base case scenario requires that an enabling environment is established to overcome barriers and mitigate risks. This scenario involves commitment from many stakeholders at country level, and a widespread sense of ownership, where decisions by all actors are made to support the desired outcome.

Paradigm Shift Scenario

The paradigm shift scenario represents a fundamental transformational change for the country, with a profound impact on the national energy matrix and on the sector's business models. Targets sought in the paradigm shift scenario go beyond the conditional contributions in the current NDC. This scenario will result in 52% of fossil fuels reduced compared to a business-as-usual situation. The decision to pursue this scenario can be made any time before 2023 when the SAP targets are expected to be achieved. This decision could go hand in hand with a second NDC establishing more ambitious emission reduction targets for 2030. The paradigm shift scenario requires a strengthened policy framework and a well-functioning financial scheme duly considering the challenges and risks associated with the nationwide transformation. This scenario will make Maldives an exemplary case of the fight against global warming for the rest of Asia and the world.

2.6   Results

In both scenarios, it is expected that by 2023, 70% of the maximum electricity day demand in inhabited islands, except the islands in the Greater Male' Region, is supplied with renewable energies. The Greater Male' Region faces additional technical and economic barriers for increasing the production of electricity from renewable energy. For the Greater Male' Region, the base case scenario aims to achieve 20% of the maximum electricity day demand, and the paradigm shift scenario 30% by 2023. Results expected for 2030 are shown in Table 7.

Table 7: Road Map Results for Year 2030
(compared to business as usual)

Subsector	Base Case Scenario	Paradigm Shift Scenario
Electricity: Energy efficiency	• 10% in all inhabited islands and in resorts, industrial, and agricultural islands	• 20% in the Greater Male' Region; 15% in other inhabited islands; and 20% in resorts, industrial, and agricultural islands
Electricity: Renewable energy	• 21% renewable energy share in electricity production o 13% in the Greater Male' Region o 39% in other inhabited islands o 15% in resorts, industrial, and agricultural islands	• 44% renewable energy share in electricity production o 38% in the Greater Male' Region o 48% in other inhabited islands o 50% in resorts, industrial, and agricultural islands
Sea and road transport	• 22% fuel use reduction in sea transport • 22% fuel use reduction in road transport	• 42% fuel use reduction in sea transport • 52% fuel use reduction in road transport
Cooking	• 35% LPG replaced with electricity (induction stoves)	• 50% LPG replaced with electricity (induction stoves)
Total fossil fuels saved	• 30% diesel reduced • 22% petrol reduced • 35% LPG reduced **=>29% fossil fuels reduced**	• 52% diesel reduced • 52% petrol reduced • 50% LPG reduced **=>52% fossil fuels reduced**

LPG = liquefied petroleum gas.
Source: Asian Development Bank.

The total fossil fuel consumption of the country in 2030 (diesel, petrol, and LPG) would be reduced by 29% (compared to business as usual) in the base case scenario, and by 52% in the paradigm shift scenario. In absolute values, in the absence of measures (business as usual), the consumption of fossil fuels is expected to grow from 674,000 tons in 2020 to 1,223,000 tons in 2030. The base case scenario forecasts that fuel consumption grows only to 864,000 tons, and the paradigm shift scenario forecasts 583,000 tons of fossil fuels in 2030. This is a net reduction of 13.5% compared to present consumption. The expected trajectories for the consumption of fossil fuels is presented in Figure 6.

In terms of energy efficiency in the electricity sector, the base case scenario aims to achieve in 2030 a 10% energy efficiency target, compared to business as usual, in all inhabited islands and in resorts, industrial, and agricultural islands. The paradigm shift scenario sets a 20% target for the Greater Male' Region; 13% for the rest of inhabited islands; and 20% for resorts, industrial, and agricultural islands.

In terms of electricity produced by renewable energy sources, the base case scenario aims to achieve in 2030 a 13% share in the Greater Male' Region; 39% in the rest of inhabited islands; and 15% in resorts, industrial, and agricultural islands. The paradigm shift scenario proposes a transformational change in the country's energy matrix and how the sector's investments are made. This scenario aims to achieve in 2030 a 38% share in the Greater Male' Region; 48% in the rest of inhabited islands; and 50% in resorts, industrial, and agricultural islands.

Figure 6: Forecast of Fossil Fuels Consumed (Diesel + Petrol + Liquefied Petroleum Gas) under Two Road Map Scenarios Compared to Business as Usual
('000 tons)

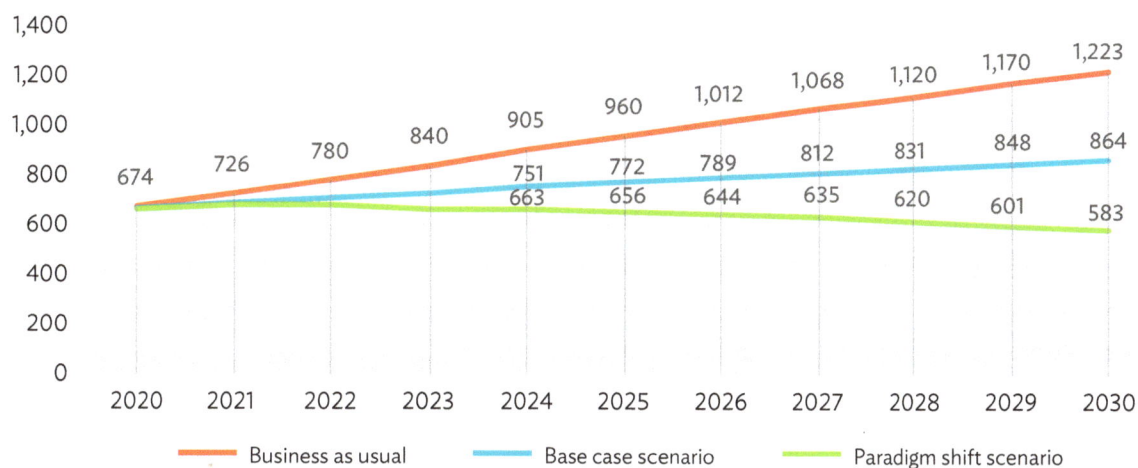

	2020	2021	2022	2023	2024	2025	2026	2027	2028	2029	2030
Business as usual	674	726	780	840	905	960	1,012	1,068	1,120	1,170	1,223
Base case scenario					751	772	789	812	831	848	864
Paradigm shift scenario					663	656	644	635	620	601	583

Source: Asian Development Bank.

For the transport subsector, the base case scenario forecasts that by 2030, 22% diesel and petrol is reduced in intra-islands sea transport and in road transport (compared to business as usual). The paradigm shift scenario sets a target of 42% diesel reduction in sea transport and 52% petrol reduction in road transport.

In the case of LPG use in cooking, the base case scenario forecasts that by 2030, 35% of LPG demand is reduced (compared to business as usual), while the paradigm shift scenario expects a 50% reduction.

2.7 Alignment with Sustainable Development Goals

This Road Map is fully aligned with several United Nations' Sustainable Development Goals (SDGs). The important level of foreseen investments in renewable energy infrastructure by this Road Map has its most direct impact on SDG 7 (affordable and clean energy), SDG 12 (responsible consumption and production), SDG 13 (climate action), and SDG 14 (life below water). This Road Map has an important positive effect on the conservation of oceans and life below water since it stops the uncontrolled growth of fossil fuel transportation by boats and possible spills this activity sometimes causes.

In relation to the use of renewable energy for the production of drinking water on the islands, the key feature relevant to the SDGs is the improved efficiency in groundwater management. The United Nations University Institute for Water, Environment and Health (UNU-INWEH), in partnership with the International Water Management Institute (IWMI) and the CGIAR Research Program on Water,

Land and Ecosystems (WLE), have recently concluded positive interlinkages between sustainable use of groundwater and SDG 6 (clean water and sanitation), SDG 12 (responsible consumption and production), and SDG 13 (climate action).[12]

The implementation of this Road Map also has clear socioeconomic impacts on SDG 1 (no poverty), SDG 3 (good health and well-being), SDG 5 (gender equality), SDG 8 (decent work and economic growth), SDG 9 (industry, innovation, and infrastructure), SDG 10 (reduced inequalities), and SDG 11 (sustainable cities and communities). For example, the installation of PV panels and small wind turbines on rooftops will empower the excluded sector of the population, thus reducing inequality. In relation with gender inclusiveness, the Government of Maldives is fully committed to achieve equality. To this aim, several important actions are being carried out by the government under the POISED project:

1. Training and consultations on gender inclusiveness and renewable energy advocacy for more than 600 participants on 91 islands were held.
2. Awareness campaigns on gender inclusiveness and renewable energy addressed to the communities were conducted on 111 islands. Similar campaigns are planned for additional 51 islands.
3. Sensitization sessions on gender inclusiveness and renewable energy addressed to the Women Development Committees (WDCs) were conducted on 49 islands.
4. Ice-making factories will be installed on four islands to be managed by island councils in partnership with WDCs. This initiative will boost livelihood in fisheries communities and become an income generation possibility for the councils and the WDCs. Such intervention is particularly relevant in a time when the tourism industry is under pressure due to the COVID-19 pandemic.
5. Renewable energy and career guidance sessions for school children including parents and teachers for Grades 8–12 were conducted on 109 islands covering a total of 6,745 students (3,292 female students and 3,453 male students). These sessions were eye-opening for parents, teachers, and students about renewable energy as a potential career path, higher education, and training. Similar guidance sessions are planned for additional 51 islands.
6. Enterprises run by women will be supported with 2–3 kW solar systems to reduce their energy costs and help them achieve economic viability.

The implementation of this Road Map will also have an impact on SDG 2 (zero hunger), since competitive and reliable renewable energy in industrial and agricultural islands promote the cultivation of crops during the whole year. Altogether, the road map implementation will greatly help Maldives drive its economic growth sustainably, reducing inequality, poverty, and food insecurity.

[12] L. Guppy et al. 2018. Groundwater and Sustainable Development Goals: Analysis of Interlinkages. *UNU-INWEH Report Series*. Issue 04. Hamilton, Canada: United Nations University Institute for Water, Environment and Health. https://inweh.unu.edu/wp-content/uploads/2018/12/Groundwater-and-Sustainable-Development-Goals-Analysis-of-Interlinkages.pdf.

3 SECTOR ASSESSMENT

3.1 Fuel Imports

Imported fossil fuels are by large the most important source of energy for the entire country. Fuel imports account for about 10% of Maldives' GDP; approximately half of the fuel imports is for electricity generation. It is estimated that, in 2019, Maldives imported 723,000 tons of refined petroleum products (Figure 7), used for the following purposes:[13]

- Diesel is used for electricity generation, industries (fisheries and water desalination), and sea transport.
- Petrol is used mostly for road transport.
- LPG is used for cooking and water heating. LPG is rapidly displacing the use of biomass as the main source of energy for domestic purposes in small inhabited islands.
- Aviation fuel is used by the aviation sector.
- Diesel, LPG, and aviation fuel are shipped to all inhabited islands and resorts islands. Logistically, this is very cumbersome and costly to operate.

Figure 7: Fuel Imports by Maldives in 2019
(tons)

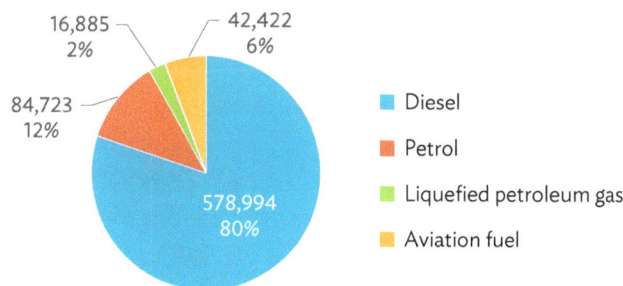

16,885
2%

42,422
6%

84,723
12%

578,994
80%

- Diesel
- Petrol
- Liquefied petroleum gas
- Aviation fuel

Source: Maldives Customs Service. Total Imports 2019. https://www.customs.gov.mv/Media/Documents/downloads (accessed 24 July 2020).

---

13   Maldives Customs Service. Total Imports 2019. https://www.customs.gov.mv/Media/Documents/downloads (accessed 24 July 2020).

3.2 Electricity Subsector

Electricity Supply

Inhabited islands in Maldives have a total installed capacity of about 290 MW diesel generators in 186 powerhouses, and more than 22 MW in renewable energy installations in 186 powerhouses (Figure 8). The FENAKA Corporation Ltd. operates 148 powerhouses; the State Electric Company Ltd. (STELCO) operates 35 powerhouses, including all those located in the Greater Male' Region; the Male' Water and Sewerage Company Pvt. Ltd. (MWSC) operates 1 powerhouse at R. Dhuvaafaru; and the rest are operated by the island councils. Resorts islands have an additional 144 MW of power generation capacity (which are managed independently of the government) and industrial islands have about 20 MW of power generation capacity.[14]

Figure 8: Evolution of Renewable Energy Installations in Maldives
(kilowatt)

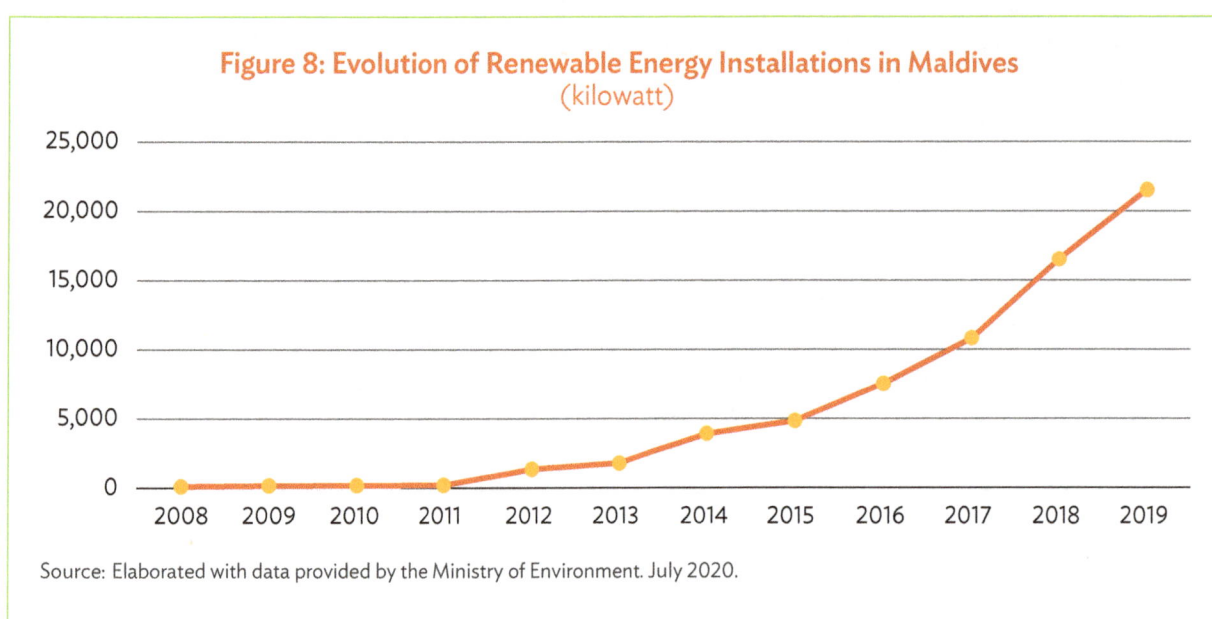

Source: Elaborated with data provided by the Ministry of Environment. July 2020.

Universal access to electricity was achieved in all of Maldives in 2008. But despite this great accomplishment, Maldives has one of the highest-cost power generation in South Asia. The reason is that electricity is produced mainly by diesel generators. The imported fuel is shipped in small quantities by boat to each island across the country, which can make fuel notably more expensive. The cost of electricity production is unaffordable, from $0.19/kWh to $0.70/kWh, depending on the size and efficiency of the electricity system. The most efficient diesel generators in Maldives produce electricity at a cost ranging between $0.23/kWh and $0.33/kWh, while for many of the smaller inhabited islands, costs can be as high as $0.70/kWh (footnote 14).

---

[14] World Bank Group. 2020a. *Project Appraisal Document of the Accelerating Sustainable Private Investments in Renewable Energy (ASPIRE) Project.* Report No. 145392-MV. Washington, DC.

Annual subsidies to the electricity sector currently amount to Rf1 billion ($65 million at the end of 2019). Subsidies is one of four areas identified by the government for stricter expenditure management. Both STELCO and FENAKA rely heavily on government's subsidies. Fuel subsidy accounted for the volatility in fuel prices and made up about 65% of the direct subsidy budget in 2018. It is applied if the fuel cost per liter is above a threshold baseline rate. The difference between the market price and baseline rate is then paid off directly to the State Trading Organization (STO) as a subsidy to allow the utilities to purchase fuel from STO at a lower price. Usage subsidy accounts for about 35% of latest direct subsidy budget, to be paid to the utilities to compensate an adjustment for harmonizing domestic and business category tariffs across all islands (footnote 14). As a consequence, despite 100% accessibility, energy supply becomes expensive and the country cannot guarantee energy security.

1. Greater Male' Region

In 2019, the power generation installed capacity in the Greater Male' Region was 149.6 MW of diesel generators operated by STELCO. These power plants produced 488 GWh (Table 8).

Table 8: Electricity Production by Diesel Power Plants in the Greater Male' Region, 2019

Subsector	Installed Capacity (megawatt)	Electricity Produced (gigawatt-hour)
Male'	81.4	386
Hulhumale'	62	81
Villingili	4	14
Thilafushi and Gulhifalhu	2.2	7
Total	**149.6**	**488**

Source: Elaborated with data provided by the State Electric Company Ltd. (STELCO) and the Ministry of Environment. July 2020.

The installation of rooftop solar PV panels in the Greater Male' Region has increased in the past 5 years reaching more than 3,000 kWp at the beginning of 2020. Rooftop solar PV panels are installed by private citizens benefitting from a net-metering tariff scheme, or by the private sector after signing power purchase agreements (PPAs) with STELCO. The STELCO's Six Island Solar PV Project was the first project in Maldives completed under a PPA signed between STELCO and Renewable Energy Maldives (REM). A total of 652 kWp PV panels were installed in six different islands—K.Villingilli, K.Guraidhoo, K.Himmafushi, K.Maafushi, K.Kaashidhoo, and K.Thulusdhoo—all of them are located in the Male' Atoll.

The World Bank's Accelerating Sustainable Private Investments in Renewable Energy (ASPIRE) project supports the installations of solar PV panel through PPA contracts with STELCO. The ASPIRE project initiated its activities in 2014. One of its specific objectives was to mitigate risks for the private sector interested in investing in renewable energy in the Greater Male' Region. ASPIRE aims to bring in private sector investments in rooftop PV in the service areas of public utilities. A PPA contract supported by ASPIRE for 1.5 MW of rooftop solar PV in Hulhumale' has been operational since March 2018. A private project developer was awarded as an independent power producer (IPP) through an international competitive tendering. The IPP sells electricity to STELCO at a fixed price of $0.21/kWh under a 20-year PPA. This price is lower than the all-in cost of diesel-based power generation in Maldives (footnote 14). A second project supported by ASPIRE was tendered in 2019. The PPA is expected to be signed with the winner of this tender by the end of 2020. In this second project, a fixed price of $0.109/kWh for 15 years with a capital cost buy down component was offered by the project winner. This is a significantly lower tariff compared to the other PPA.

Rooftop Solar Photovoltaic. A 100 kilowatt-peak solar PV system was installed at Maldives Center for Social Education in Male' (photo by Ministry of Environment).

2. Other inhabited islands

The power generation capacity installed in other inhabited islands was about 120 MW in 2019. The large number of isolated and small dispersed islands has resulted in the development of small power systems with limited possibilities of interconnection for the majority of them.

These power systems are often oversized due to suspected demand growth. Consequently, power systems run at very low loads during off-peak hours. Operations at low loads mean poor fuel efficiency and higher costs of maintenance. Their average specific fuel consumption is particularly high, with often two or more generation sets running all the time at low load. The average specific consumption in these islands is 0.42 liter/kWh, with some islands operating close to 0.70 liter/kWh. These values are much larger than acceptable average rates for isolated systems operating with no flexibility options such as energy storage, usually marked at 0.35 liter/kWh. To transform the existing diesel-based energy systems of at least 160 islands into hybrid solar PV-diesel systems, Maldives established the Preparing Outer Islands for Sustainable Energy Development (POISED) project in 2014 with ADB's support. POISED is a flagship action that aims to transform current diesel-based generation in islands into hybrid renewable energy mini-grid systems. These hybrid systems include PV power plants, battery energy storage systems, energy management systems, and efficient diesel generation sets. POISED includes distribution network upgrades to allow high levels of renewable energy penetration. The architecture for the hybrid grids has three categories:

- **Type A.** Islands with moderate renewable energy penetration (less than 40% of peak load) and no energy storage.
- **Type B.** Islands with high renewable energy penetration (40% to 100% of the peak load) where battery storage provides grid-support services.
- **Type C.** Islands with very high renewable energy penetration (Beyond 100% of peak load) where a battery storage typically allows the system to operate 4 to 6 hours with no diesel generation sets.

POISED is the largest energy sector intervention for Maldives in four phases covering at least 160 inhabited islands within all 20 atolls across the country, with a target of 28.8 MWp solar PV installations (Figure 9).

Implementation of the POISED project has led to important results and findings. The concept design of hybrid systems (efficient diesel generators + solar PV plants + energy storage) has resulted in success for Maldives. solar PV with storage has proven suitable and competitive for the high penetration of renewable energy in Maldives (POISED type B projects), with an average fuel savings of 25%. Additional funding for phase 5 in 2023 may cover additional 28 islands with 5.5 MWp in solar PV installations.

In relation to gender equality and inclusiveness, the POISED project has put great emphasis on the empowerment of women in the energy sector to reduce the gap in equal access of women to economic resources and higher education. The POISED project has engaged in awareness campaigns, training, and consultation on gender inclusiveness and green economy in most of the 160 islands targeted. In partnership with island councils and the Women Development Committees (WDCs), POISED is installing ice-making factories on four islands to make them an income opportunity for women. This initiative is particularly relevant in a time when the tourism industry is under pressure due to the COVID-19 pandemic. To increase female representation in the renewable energy technical field, POISED has trained the female staff at the utilities. Career guidance sessions related to renewable energy as a potential career path addressed to school children in grades 8–12 have also been conducted on 109 islands, and similar sessions are planned for an additional 51 islands.

Figure 9: Installation of Hybrid Systems in Maldives by the POISED Project

TYPE	ISLANDS	BATTERY	PV PENETRATION	FUEL SAVING
A	5	✖	<40	10
B	128	✔	>40 <100	23
C	27	✔	>100	39

out of 200 inhabited islands | | % of daily peak load | % , on already operating islands

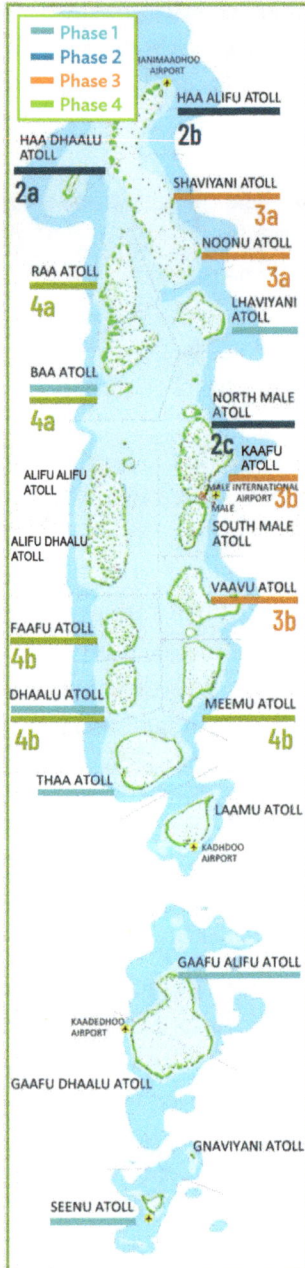

Legend:
- Phase 1
- Phase 2
- Phase 3
- Phase 4

Total installed capacity by the POISED project

Solar PV:	**11.2 MWp**
Diesel generators:	**11.6 MW**
Batteries:	**5.7 MWh**

Phase 1 (completed)
- 2.3 MWp installed in 5 islands

Phase 2 (ongoing)
- 2.3 MWp installed in 14 islands (phase 2b)
- The European Investment Bank (EIB) support planned for 3.5 MWp in 13 islands (phase 2a)

Phase 3 (ongoing)
- 3.0 MWp installed in 27 islands (phase 3a)
- The EIB support planned for 2.9 MWp in 25 islands (phase 3b)

Phase 4 (ongoing)
- The EIB support planned for 11.2 MWp in 45 islands (phases 4a and 4b)

PV installed under counterpart funding
- 3.6 MWp installed in 33 islands

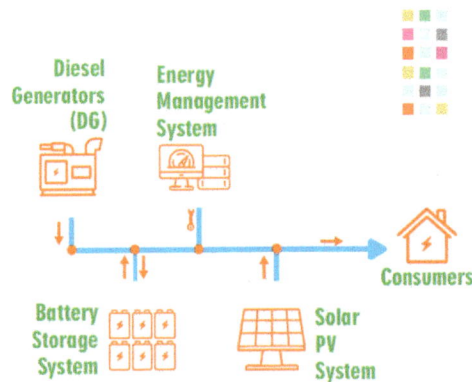

GENERAL POWER SYSTEM ARCHITECTURE

EIB = European Investment Bank, MWh = megawatt-hour, MWp = megawatt-peak, POISED = Preparing Outer Islands for Sustainable Energy Development, PV = photovoltaic.

Source: Information provided by the POISED project and the Ministry of Environment. March 2020.

■ **POISED = Preparing Outer Islands for Sustainable Energy Development Project.** The POISED project has demonstrated significant physical progress with the installation of 1,600 kilowatts-peak (kWp) Solar photovoltaic system in Addu City, S. Hithadhoo at phase 1 (left) and 200 kWp in Kelaa, Haa Ali at phase 2 (right) (photos by Ministry of Environment).

3.   Desalination plants, industry, and agriculture

Maldives aims at an integrated water resource management (IWRM) approach based on cost-effective adaptation measures. In such approach, availability, reliability, and affordability of fresh water is supported by desalination systems. Water desalination was brought to Male' city in the 1980s. It was later introduced in other high densely populated islands because of the huge damage caused by the 2004 tsunami to groundwater aquifers and storage facilities. According to Maldives' latest census (2014), 30% of drinking water in Male' and 7% in smaller inhabited islands come from desalination plants. Desalination plants use diesel generators for their operation. The government constructs desalination plants and transfers them to FENAKA to operate them and provide water services. Regulated water tariffs are not sufficient to cover diesel costs, leading to huge losses.

The fishing industry is Maldives' second largest economic sector and an intensive user of refrigeration. Compared to 2017, there was a growth of 5.5% in fish catch during 2018. Out of the total fish catch in 2018, 43.5% was exported. The latest census in Maldives (2014) found that there were, at the time, 22 operating fishing enterprises. Most of them generated their own electricity with diesel generator sets. Maldives also has six islands leased for agricultural purposes.

4.   Resort islands

As for the resort islands, the typical diesel power generation installed capacity is 900 kW. These powerhouses operate intermittently when the islands are operating for their guests. Currently, only 23 resorts comply with submitting their power generation information to the Ministry of Environment. This makes it difficult to properly assess the total installed capacity in these islands and their fuel usage.

Awareness of the Benefits of Energy Efficiency

Energy consumption in buildings and households accounts for a large share of the total end use of energy in Maldives. However, there are no data available on their energy consumption and their levels of energy efficiency. Most buildings in Maldives suffer from large energy losses. The majority of residential buildings have been designed for the use of fans as the source of comfort air. These buildings later adopted air-conditioners. Unfortunately, not many dwellings are designed to keep comfortable room temperatures. Inefficient lighting and household appliances are additional factors for the low levels of energy efficiency in Maldives' buildings.

Energy inefficiencies in Maldives' buildings and households are mainly due to the lack of adequate construction and refurbishment materials, the lack of data and technical knowledge, and misinformation or ineffective communication to key players and stakeholders. The necessary information for monitoring is also lacking; for instance, technical records of imported equipment are nonexistent. The data regularly recorded by Maldives Custom Services do not capture information related to the capacity and technology of products imported, the energy rating, and the models and make, among others. Technical specifications for imported equipment are needed. There is also no reporting of product sales and technology in place by retailers and importers to any national regulatory agency. Without this information, it is difficult to inform the population on the benefits of using energy-efficient equipment, or to monitor the results of any related campaign.

To address these issues, the Ministry of Environment established the Low-Carbon Energy Island Strategies (LCEI) project to promote energy-efficient practices (Table 9). The project is funded by the Global Environment Facility and supported by the UN Environment Programme (UNEP).

Table 9: Relevant Activities Initiated by the Low-Carbon Energy Island Strategies Project

Low-carbon energy islands activities	Elaboration of a baseline to assess the characteristics of imported appliances.
	Development of the Standards and Labeling Program.
	Development of an energy and water saving guideline for retrofits and new buildings.
	Development of a buildings certification system.
	Introduction of Green Building concepts in Maldives National University curricula.

Source: Government of Maldives, Ministry of Environment. March 2020.

Forecasted Demand Growth (Business as Usual)

With no relevant interventions to reduce the consumption of fossil fuels in the electricity subsector, the aggregated maximum day demand in Maldives will grow from 301 MW in 2020 to 508 MW in 2030 (Figure 10).

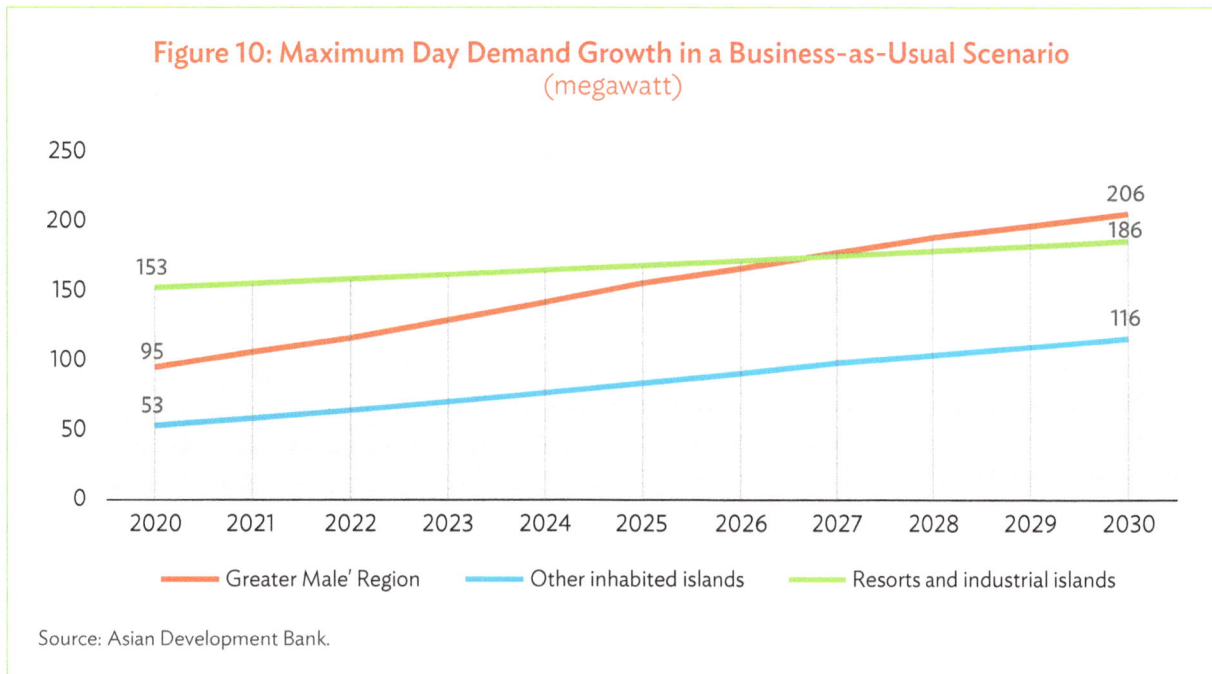

Figure 10: Maximum Day Demand Growth in a Business-as-Usual Scenario
(megawatt)

Source: Asian Development Bank.

In terms of electricity consumption, Figure 11 shows the resulting forecast for the Greater Male' Region; other inhabited islands; and resorts, industrial, and agricultural islands. Electricity consumption in Maldives has been forecasted for this Road Map to grow from 1,494 GWh in 2020 to 2,665 GWh in 2030, according to the following assumptions:

- Greater Male' Region: Average of 10% demand growth until 2025 and thereafter, an average of 6% growth until 2030.
- Other inhabited islands: Average of 9% demand growth until 2027 and thereafter, an average of 6% growth until 2030.
- The combined growth of resorts, industrial, and agricultural islands for 2020 is estimated at 0% and 2% from 2021 onward. Slowdown in tourism activities and larger support to industrial and agricultural islands due to the COVID-19 pandemic are considered in this forecast.

Figure 11: Electricity Consumption Growth in a Business-as-Usual Scenario
(gigawatt-hour)

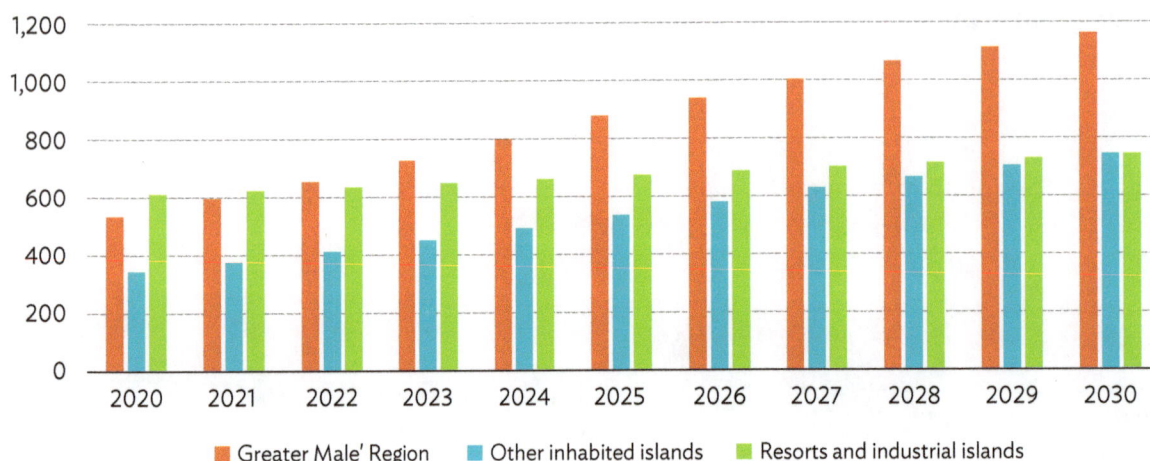

Source: Asian Development Bank.

3.3 Transport Subsector

Fuel Supply

1. Sea transport

The country's isolation and highly scattered population makes transport of people, goods, and services fuel-intensive and very expensive. While all inhabited islands are served by a basic nationwide transportation network of ferries and jetties, connectivity across the low-lying islands needs to be improved to sustain the development efforts of Maldives.

The estimated consumption of diesel fuel used in sea transport has grown at a rapid pace in the past decade. Between 2017 and 2019, the annual consumption of diesel used in vessels grew from 149,000 tons to 195,000 tons. The number of registered vessels has increased in the period 2010–2018 from 9,687 to 14,003. In particular, the number of Dhonis for passenger's transportation has increased from 5,840 to 7,246 in this period (footnote 2). However, there is no information on the energy efficiency of these vessels.

A pilot test for a public transport ferry powered with 100% renewable energy is currently considered for financing under the POISED project.

2. Land transport

A large part of the fuel used in land transportation is consumed in the Greater Male' Region and in Addu City. Other inhabited islands and resorts, industrial, and agricultural islands also have vehicles, though they are lower in number.

The estimated consumption of petrol used in road transport also grew at a rapid pace in the past decade. Between 2017 and 2019, the annual consumption of petrol used in road transport grew from 58,000 tons to 85,000 tons. The number of registered vehicles has more than doubled in the period 2010–2018, from 46,028 to 108,532. Motorcycles account for 83% of all vehicles with an active registration in 2018 (footnote 2). Same as with vessels, there is no information on the year of manufacturing, efficiency, and amount of CO_2 emissions of registered road vehicles.

Forecasted Demand Growth (Business as Usual)

The consumption of diesel for sea transport in 2020 is assumed to remain the same as in 2019 (195,000 tons) due to the COVID-19 pandemic. It is estimated that it will then grow to 383,000 tons in 2030. Fuel consumption in road transport (mostly petrol) will grow from 85,000 tons in 2020 to 138,000 tons in 2030 (Figure 12). The assumptions made in this forecast are:

- sea transport: average of 10% growth until 2025 and thereafter, an average of 5% growth until 2030; and
- road transport: average of 5% growth until 2030.

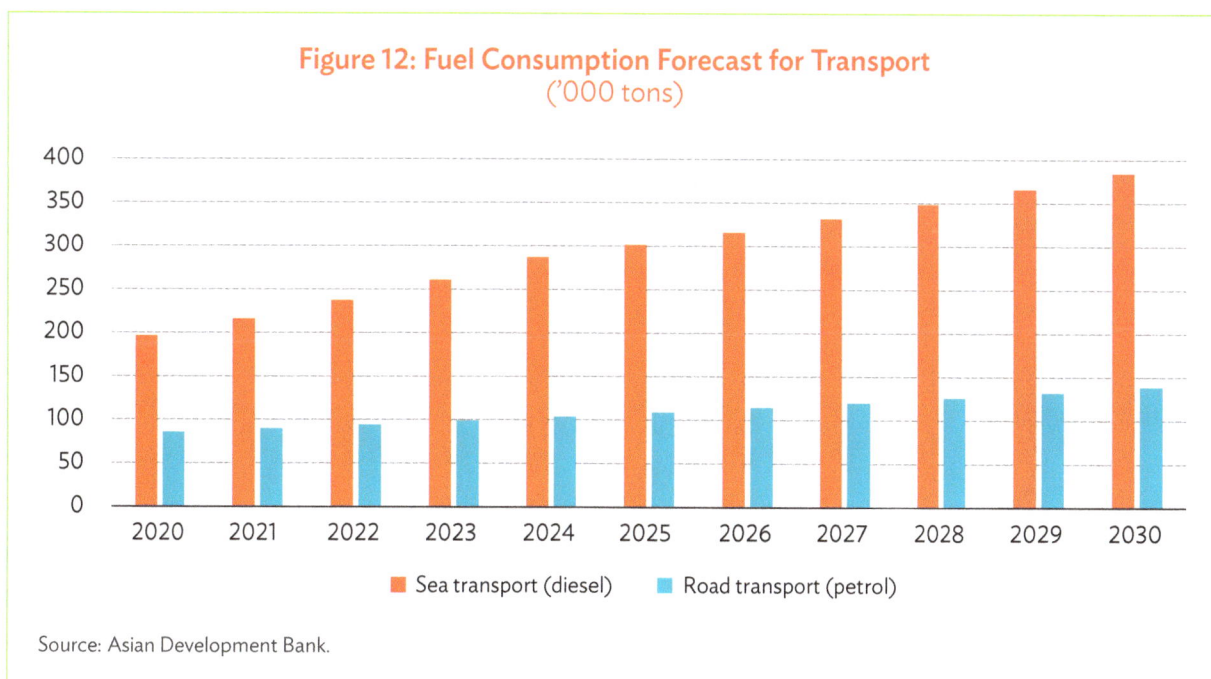

Figure 12: Fuel Consumption Forecast for Transport
('000 tons)

Source: Asian Development Bank.

3.4   Liquefied Petroleum Gas for Cooking Subsector

Supply and Forecasted Demand Growth (Business as Usual)

Most of the liquefied petroleum gas (LPG) imported by the country is used in cooking. LPG imports have grown from 14,483 tons in 2017 to 16,885 tons in 2019 (footnote 2). LPG is distributed in standard LPG bottles to the final consumer. With no relevant interventions to reduce the consumption of LPG in cooking, the demand of LPG is expected to grow at an average rate of 4% until it reaches 25,000 tons in 2030 (Figure 13).

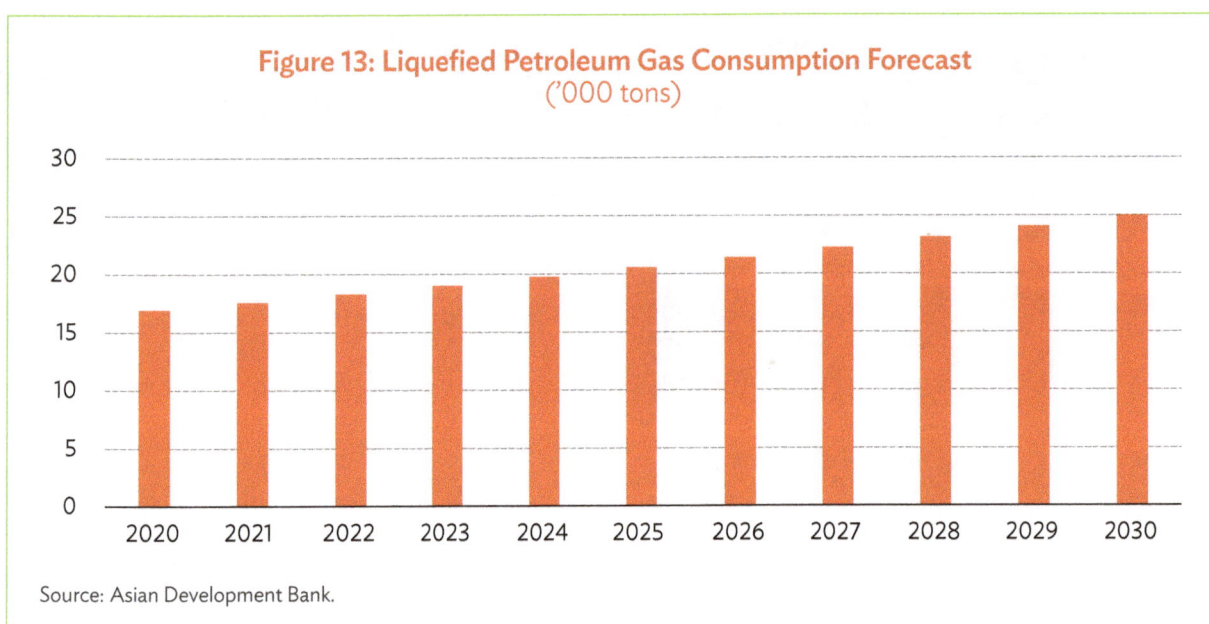

Figure 13: Liquefied Petroleum Gas Consumption Forecast
('000 tons)

Source: Asian Development Bank.

3.5   Risks and Barriers

Maldives faces many risks and barriers in transiting toward a low-carbon energy sector. These risks and barriers must be addressed when realizing the sector's vision and implementing this Road Map, since they can quickly affect the security and affordability of energy supply, and in turn, impact the country's economy.

Economic Risks

Several economic insecurity issues are associated with the import of fossil fuels. The small amount of imports tendered does not facilitate price competition. As a consequence, many importers in Maldives do not benefit from credit terms that importers from larger countries do. Most international suppliers give a 45-day credit to Maldives' importers, and very few offer a 90-day credit. In addition, the tankers used by Maldives' companies are too small (maximum of 24,000 metric tons) to use facilities in the neighboring South Asia region and negotiate lower freight rates. These ports lack berthing facilities for such small tankers. Even the closest port to Maldives, Cochin in India, caters to tankers of not less than 30,000 deadweight tonnage (DWT). As a consequence, Maldives' importers are forced to make special arrangements through the United Arab Emirates, Malaysia, or Singapore. Tankers navigate one way with cargo and make the return trip with ballast. This means extra freight costs for Maldives' companies.

Maldives is highly dependent on foreign imports for almost all goods, including staple food items, electronics and appliances, and other necessities. Imported goods are transported to all islands by boats that run on diesel. Therefore, the prices of imported fuels and the volatility of those prices have a direct and strong impact on the country's economy. Rising fuel prices could lead to Maldives' economic and social instability, since they reduce the country's capacity to invest in creating jobs, improve health care and education, and introduce new farming practices to keep yields up in times of food insecurity.

Regulatory Barriers

Despite the positive evolution of the energy sector policy, some regulatory barriers remain. With the new amended net-metering regulation, individuals installing renewable energy on their rooftops will be paid within 6 months for excess units generated from home solar PV systems. However, regulatory barriers remain in regard to remuneration mechanisms for larger installations.

Schemes that can be considered in the future include auctioning systems and feed-in tariffs, as well as improving the guidelines for PPAs. Policy directions are also needed for resorts to scale-up renewable energy infrastructure and implement ambitious energy efficiency programs.

Technical standards for the provision of ancillary services by energy storage shall be developed, including technical standards for electric vehicles. Efforts should be oriented toward developing tariffs for smart charging of electric vehicles (i.e., establishing incentives for charging during low demand hours or during periods with excess renewable energy production).

Experience with Innovative Technologies

Utility companies owning and operating electricity production assets in Maldives have mainly implemented conventional energy projects since the beginning of the country's industrialization. They have been operating and maintaining diesel-based power plants for several years and have gained valuable experience and knowledge on such systems. When it comes to renewable energy technologies, however, they are still at the infant stage in Maldives, and there is limited knowledge and experience on their operation and maintenance.

The lack of adequate access to such technologies is a limitation that may result in wrong technology choices, deficient design of solutions (including capacity sizing, storage, control system installation, and service implementation), and non-optimal or poor configuration of energy systems. Innovative technologies may also not be sustainably implemented because of a focus on hardware only, ignoring the "softer" elements, such as know-how, experience, and capabilities. Pilot projects are needed for learning and testing the interactions of new technologies with policies, regulations, tariff methodologies, and business models.

Since the private sector is reluctant to assume the risks associated with new technologies, stronger support and intervention of the government and development partners is needed to leapfrog to more competitive positions and give Maldives the opportunity to reach its sector's vision faster.

Resilience to the Impacts of Climate Change

Maldives is at the forefront of the most vulnerable countries to the impacts of climate change. Its high vulnerability stems from the geographical characteristics of the islands—their small size, low elevation, and scattered distribution in a large ocean area. These distinctive characteristics have led to the establishment of the country's critical infrastructure within 100 meters from the coastline. These include powerhouses, drinking water plants, medical centers, waste collection and treatment plants, and households.[15] Such proximity makes Maldives' islands very vulnerable to the many effects of climate change, including the erosion caused by sea level rise, tsunamis, extreme weather, and sea temperature rise.[16] In 1998 and in 2016, the "El Niño" phenomenon caused a significant coral bleaching of the coral reefs of Maldives. Coral reefs are not only home to thousands of fish species, hundreds of mollusks and crustacean species, and species of amphibians, whales, and dolphins; they also protect the islands from the erosive effects of the sea. Rainwater shortages are also more frequent due to the effects of climate change.[17]

The country lacks sufficient capacities and resources to respond locally, on time, and effectively to weather-related disasters. Extreme weather events disrupt, and many times, fully stop the regular supply of food, fuel, and essential goods to the islands. The small size of the islands and their lack of resources have made emergency stockpiling very difficult. High levels of community resilience are needed to prevent and combat these risks and enhance local human capacity to respond to emergencies.

Environmental and Biodiversity Protection

Maldives is globally known for its unique beauty formed by coral reefs, seagrass, mangroves, beaches, forests, and brackish lakes and ponds. These natural habitats and their rich biodiversity contribute to 89% of the national GDP and 71% of employment.[18]

---

[15] Government of Maldives, Ministry of Environment and Energy. 2016b. *Second National Communication of Maldives to the United Nations Framework Convention on Climate Change*. Male'.

[16] The 2007 IPCC report predicted that global warming will result in sea level rise of up to 59 centimeters by 2100, which means that most of the countries affected may need to be abandoned.

[17] Maldives Meteorological Services predicts an overall decreasing trend for annual rainfall over Hanimaadhoo, of 9.5 millimeters (mm); Malé, of 0.02 mm; and Gan, of 2.21 mm.

[18] Government of Maldives, Ministry of Environment and Energy. 2015b. *National Biodiversity Strategy and Action Plan of Maldives, 2016–2025*. Male'.

Both the new infrastructure and population growth exert pressure on the natural environment and biodiversity. Technology options for renewable energy are severely limited in Maldives due to non-availability of land. Land is very scarce for the installation of ground-mounted solar PV farms and wind turbines. ISO and WHO guidelines for environmental noise require that wind turbines are placed at a distance ranging from 400 to 1,500 meters from houses to reduce noise below 40 decibels (dB). In particular, the reclamation of land associated with new infrastructure projects would be potentially harmful if not done properly. Over the past 4 decades, land reclamation has resulted in over-extraction of natural resources, habitat alteration, and damage to critical ecosystems. Inadequate waste management, including the lack of adequate and effective procedures to dispose used chemicals and untreated sewerage, has increased the levels of pollution across the country—harming biodiversity and aquifers. In the absence or insufficiency of natural water supplies, the population is forced to produce larger amounts of desalinized water and import more prepared food and bottled water. This has led to larger use of fossil fuels which could significantly harm the environment and biodiversity.

4 STRATEGY FOR THE ELECTRICITY SUBSECTOR

4.1   Flagship Interventions

This Road Map foresees interventions around the three pillars of the energy sector vision: energy efficiency first, investments on renewable energy, and integration of technology innovation. Interventions in energy efficiency are grouped according to supply side interventions—generation, transmission, and distribution of electricity—and according to demand side interventions. Energy efficiency interventions in Maldives aim to reduce energy consumption and costs without lowering the quality of life in the country. Investments in renewable energy infrastructure will focus on off-the-shelf solutions, including roof solar PV, waste-to-energy, and small rooftop wind turbines. Possible synergies with water desalination plants will be considered. Integration of technology innovation includes the introduction of floating PV platforms, ocean energy (tidal, wave, and ocean thermal), and energy storage using hydrogen and fuel cell technologies. Flagship interventions foreseen in this Road Map are listed in Table 10. The design and monitoring framework for the base case and paradigm shift scenarios are presented in Appendixes 1 and 2 of this report. The following sections detail these interventions for the Greater Male' Region; other inhabited islands; and resorts, industrial, and agricultural islands.

4.2   Greater Male' Region

The base case scenario for the Greater Male' Region estimates that by 2030, 10% of energy efficiency is achieved (compared to the business-as-usual situation). The paradigm shift scenario increases this target to 20%. Energy efficiency interventions will result in a reduction of the peak day demand from 206 MW to 185 MW in 2030 in the base case scenario, and 164 MW in the paradigm shift scenario (Figure 14).

The share of renewable energy in the electricity produced in 2030 is estimated at 13% in the base case scenario and 38% in the paradigm shift scenario. The electricity produced from renewable energy in 2030 is estimated at 144 GWh versus 962 GWh from diesel in the base case scenario, and 374 GWh from renewable energy versus 610 GWh from diesel in the paradigm shift scenario (Figures 15 and 16). The approximate investments needed in new renewable energy infrastructure, including the costs of distribution grid upgrade and storage, are 120 million in the best case scenario, and $260 million in the paradigm shift scenario.

Table 10: Road Map Interventions for the Electricity Subsector

Energy efficiency—Supply side
- Refurbishment of diesel generation sets
- Dual (gas or diesel) fuels for new large generation sets
- Interconnection of islands
- Reduction of electricity distribution losses

Energy efficiency—Demand side
- Efficiency in the built environment (climatization and lighting)
- Efficient domestic appliances

Renewable energy infrastructure
- Solar photovoltaic on roofs, bridges, and other structures
- Wind energy (onshore and small rooftop wind turbines)
- Waste to energy

Integration of technology innovation
- Floating solar platforms
- Ocean energy
- Energy storage using hydrogen and fuel cells technology

Source: Asian Development Bank.

Figure 14: Forecast of the Peak Day Demand in the Greater Male' Region
(megawatt)

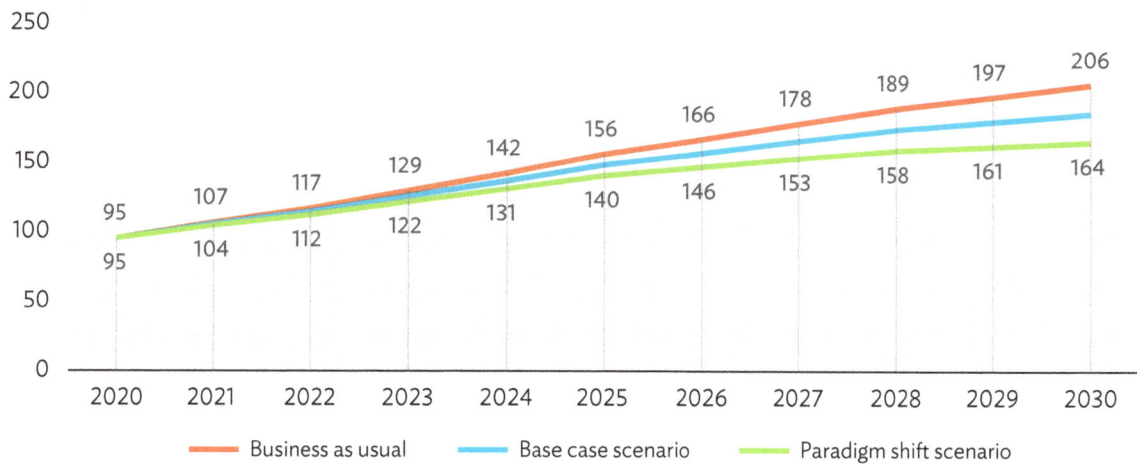

Business as usual — Base case scenario — Paradigm shift scenario

Source: Asian Development Bank.

Figure 15: Forecast of Electricity Production in the Greater Male' Region—Base Case Scenario
(gigawatt-hour)

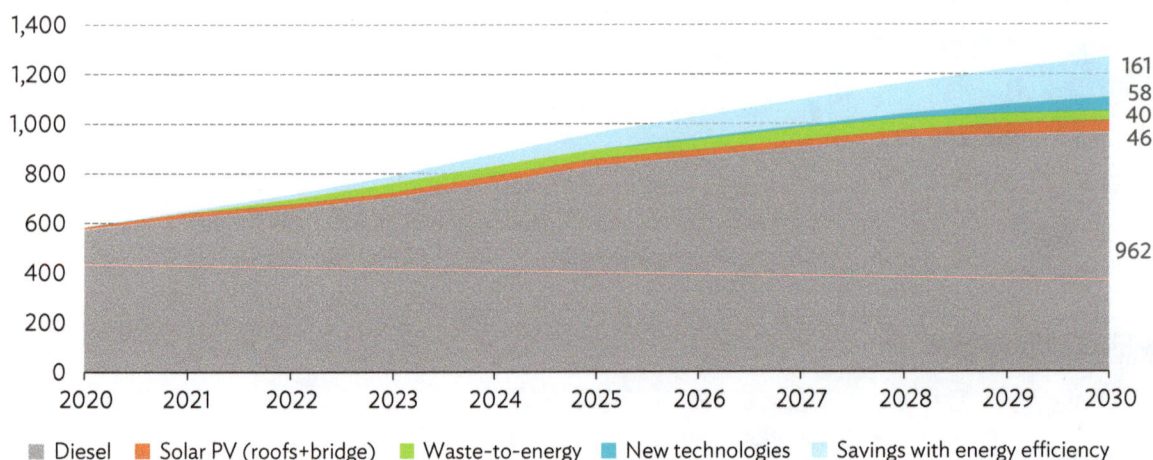

Diesel ■ Solar PV (roofs+bridge) ■ Waste-to-energy ■ New technologies ■ Savings with energy efficiency

PV = photovoltaic.
Source: Asian Development Bank.

Figure 16: Forecast of Electricity Production in the Greater Male' Region—Paradigm Shift Scenario
(gigawatt-hour)

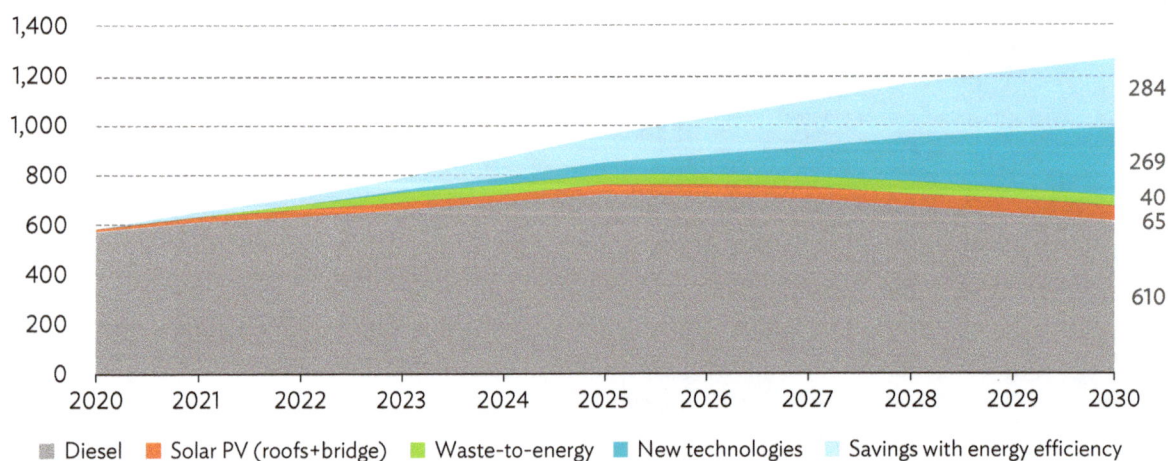

Diesel ■ Solar PV (roofs+bridge) ■ Waste-to-energy ■ New technologies ■ Savings with energy efficiency

PV = photovoltaic.
Source: Asian Development Bank.

Achieving these targets will result in a reduction of 71,000 tons of diesel consumption in the base case scenario in 2030, and 145,000 tons of diesel in the paradigm shift scenario. This is equivalent to 26% reduction for the base case scenario and 53% reduction for the paradigm shift scenario, when compared with a business-as-usual situation (Figure 17). The interventions considered for the Greater Male' Region are described in the next paragraphs.

Figure 17: Forecast of Diesel Use in Electricity Production in the Greater Male' Region
('000 tons)

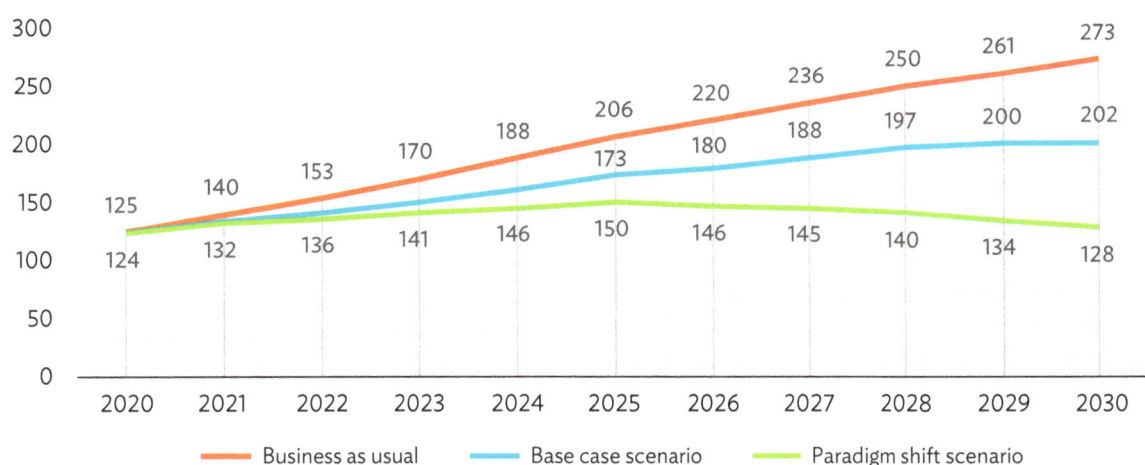

Business as usual — Base case scenario — Paradigm shift scenario

Source: Asian Development Bank.

Energy Efficiency—Supply Side

1. Dual fuel choice for new generators

The two large power plants to be commissioned by STELCO in the Greater Male' Region in 2023 are:

- an additional **50 MW power plant in Hulhumale'**, and
- a new **150 MW power plant in Thilafushi**, to serve the demand of the future international cargo port of Maldives that will be built in Gulhifalhu.

It is recommended that these two new power plants operate with a dual-fuel-option diesel gas, and that fuel flow meters are introduced in all power plants in the Greater Male' Region. The major drivers for the dual fuel choice are the cost reduction of electricity generation and the reduction of CO_2 emissions. Electricity produced with dual fuel engines using mainly LNG may reduce CO_2 emissions by 30 % (footnote 16). The cost for the new 150 MW power plant in Thilafushi is estimated at $300 million. As delivery and storage of LNG is critical, a feasibility study considering the options described in section 2.3 is needed. This study should at least consider the following:

- Space constraints at power plant side
- Feasibility of small-scale LNG (SSLNG) in Maldives (see section 2.3)
- Economic impacts on STELCO due to changes in the current project for the extension of the Hulhumale' power plant
- Utilization of the power produced by the future Thilafushi power plant

2.   Interconnection of power grids

A radial three-phase transmission grid interconnecting the Greater Male' Region will result in larger penetration of renewable energy sources and more efficient and redundant network that will optimize operation and reduce power losses in the interconnected system. Interconnection of power grids is, therefore, crucial for the success of this Road Map. The interconnection of the Greater Male' Region involves two phases:

- **Phase 1: Hulhulmale'–Hulhule'–Male'**, 100 MW × 2 circuits at 132 kV, estimated to be ready in early 2021 (Figure 18).
- **Phase 2: Male'–Villingili–GulhiFalhu–Thilafushi**, 100 MW × 3 circuits at 132 kV, expected in 2023.

The interconnection is proposed at 132 kV voltage level to optimize power transmission from Male'.

Figure 18: Phase 1 of the Interconnection of the Greater Male' Region

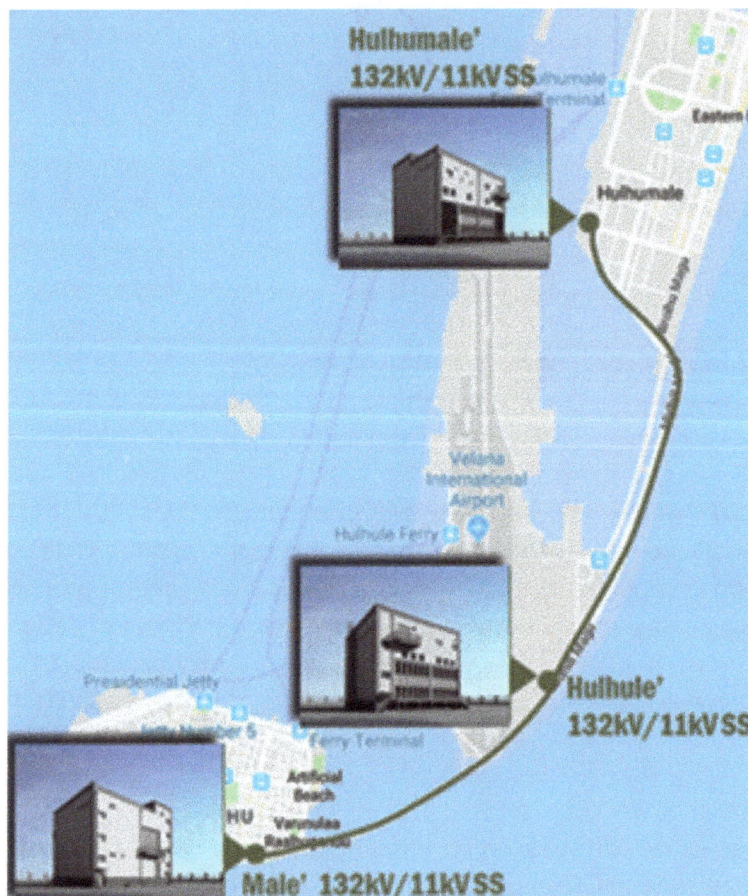

kV = kilovolt, SS = substation.
Source: Government of Maldives, State Electric Company Ltd. (STELCO). January 2020.

3. Reduction of distribution losses

A large part of distribution grids in the Greater Male' Region were not designed for the current and forecasted uses. Energy losses in these grids are a concern that must be promptly addressed. The current average loss is estimated at 8%. The upgrading of grids aims to reduce this loss to 5% by 2030.

Energy Efficiency—Demand Side

1. Energy efficiency in the built environment

The use of energy in buildings in the Greater Male' Region accounts for a large share of the total end use of electricity. Buildings are mainly categorized as residential/domestic, public buildings, and commercial buildings. The main factors that influence energy consumption in a building are climatization and lighting. Interventions related to the energy efficiency in the built environment include the following:

- **Revise and enforce building codes** to require energy efficiency and conservation measures, in particular for all public buildings and new housing developments. These building codes should also provide guidelines and promote the installation of rooftop solar PV panels for electricity production, and solar thermal for water heating.
- **Implement a certification mechanism** for energy-efficient buildings and carry out energy efficiency audits. These audits should identify the most viable options for dwelling refurbishments and should be obligatory for all public buildings and new housing developments.
- **Implement a LED street lighting program** for the Greater Male' Region.

The promotion of energy service companies (ESCOs) and the use of energy savings performance contracts (ESPCs) may facilitate the implementation of these measures.

2. Efficient lighting and domestic appliances

Efficient, automated, and centralized air-conditioning systems are not the norm in buildings. Most buildings and households use manually controlled air-conditioning units installed in each room and space to be climatized. Imports and purchases of air-conditioning units do not follow any energy performance criteria. The imports of air-conditioning units have grown from 45,000 in 2016 to 62,000 in 2019. Maldives also imports around 15,000 household refrigerators and freezers and 15,000 washing machines annually. Interventions related to efficient domestic appliances include the following:

- **Introduction of smart metering,** to measure electricity consumption as close as possible to real-time. Smart metering allows utilities to offer differentiated hourly tariffs according to the time of day and the source of energy supplied (renewable or diesel).
- **Implementation of energy efficiency labeling for electrical appliances,** in particular for air-conditioners, refrigerators, washing machines, and microwaves. The Government of Maldives, through its Ministry of Environment and Maldives Energy Authority, is working on the development of a standards and labeling program for air-conditioners, refrigerators, and washing machines.

- **Phase-out selling of inefficient lighting bulbs** used in the domestic and commercial sectors.
- **Awareness campaign** on the use of energy-efficient appliances and promotion of low-cost sensors and meters for energy efficiency.

Under the paradigm shift scenario, intervention efforts are doubled by strengthening:

- financially supported energy audits for buildings, and
- economic incentive and microcredit programs for the replacement of inefficient lighting and household appliances.

Renewable Energy Infrastructure

The base case scenario foresees the installation of 42.5 MW of conventional solar PV, wind, and waste-to-energy infrastructure in the Greater Male' Region through the private sector. The paradigm shift scenario increases this target to 61.0 MW (Table 11). The investment mechanisms chosen are power purchase agreements (PPA) for the larger infrastructure, and net-metering tariffing for small rooftop installations.

Since the Road Map's ambition is to integrate more renewable energy into the grid and to gain energy independence, some degree of industrialization of the renewable energy sector, such as introducing PV testing and PV panel assembly lines, would be advantageous for Maldives. Testing facilities at national level for renewable energy devices would ensure technical standards are maintained. Local universities can also be included in the researches done by various renewable energy companies.

Table 11: Renewable Energy Infrastructure for the Greater Male' Region, 2020–2030

| Year | Project Investment | Capacity (MW) | | Investment Mechanism |
		Base case	Paradigm shift	
2020	PV panels: Hulhule'-Male' link road	5.0	5.0	Private - PPA
2020–2023	Rooftop PV: Hulhumale'	3.0	4.0	Private – Net metering
2021–2023	Rooftop PV: Villingili	0.5	1.0	Private – Net metering
2021–2025	PV panels: Thilafushi (land and roof)	1.0	5.0	Private – PPA
2020–2030	Rooftop PV: Male'	10.0	10.0	Private – Net metering
2024–2030	Commercial rooftop PV: Gulhifalhu	10.0	18.0	Private - PPA
2022–2023	WTE plant: Thilafushi 2 x 4000 kW	8.0	8.0	Private - PPA
2026–2028	Wind turbine: Thilafushi/Gulhifalhu	2.0	2.0	Private - PPA
2024–2030	Rooftop micro wind turbines	3.0	8.0	Private – Net metering
	Total	**42.5**	**61.0**	

kW = kilowatt, MW = megawatt, PPA = power purchase agreement, PV = photovoltaic, WTE = waste-to-energy.
Source: Asian Development Bank.

1. Solar energy

- **PV panels on the Hulhumale'–Male' link road.** Sponsored by the ASPIRE project, 5.0 MWp of PV panels will be installed by the end of 2020 on the side of the road connecting Hulhumale', the international airport in Hulhule', and Male' city. Canopies are proposed to be installed on the roadsides for solar PV and allow land sites to be available for other uses. Hence, no land acquisition is required. This investment has been secured with a PPA between a private sector party and STELCO.
- **Rooftop PV panels.** The installation of rooftop PV panels in the Greater Male' Region has been successful in the past 2 years as a result of the net-metering tariffing system offered to building owners. The base case scenario estimates that up to 14.5 MWp of rooftop PV panels under net-metering tariffing conditions can be installed on Hulhumale', Male', and Thilafushi. The paradigm shift scenario increases this target to 20 MWp. PV panels are also foreseen over the roofs of the future commercial/industrial developments in Gulhifalhu. The base case scenario estimates 10 MWp of commercial rooftop PV panels, while the paradigm shift scenario estimates 18 MWp, all under a PPA arrangement.

2. Wind energy

- **Onshore wind turbine.** One wind turbine of 2 MW can be installed in Thilafushi or Gulhifalhu by 2028, under a PPA arrangement.
- **Micro rooftop wind turbine.** The base case scenario estimates that 3 MW of rooftop wind turbines can be installed under the net-metering tariffing system. This target is increased to 8 MW in the paradigm shift scenario.

3. Waste-to-energy

Power generation using municipal solid waste as fuel source has a potential for 8 MW capacity in two stages of 4 MW each on the island of Thilafushi. The first 4 MW will be installed in 2022 and the second 4 MW in 2023. Achievement of these targets requires that the interconnection with the islands of the axis Male'–Villingili–Thilafushi and Gulhifalhu is developed on time by 2022 as Thilafushi has a demand lower than 1 MW. The waste-to-energy project also requires due care to ensure that adequate pollution abatement equipment and strategy are included in this development.

Integration of Technology Innovation

The base case scenario estimates the testing and integration of innovative renewable energy technologies at 12 MW between 2026 and 2030. The paradigm shift scenario sets this target to 70 MW (Table 12). The integration of these technologies would require feasibility studies to identify the locations and technologies to be used, considering that lagoons are scarce in the Greater Male' Region.

1. Floating PV platforms

Floating PV platforms are promising for the energy mix of Maldives. The base case scenario estimates the installation of 5 MWp of floating solar during 2026–2030. The paradigm shift scenario sets this target to 30 MWp.

2. Ocean energy

Ocean energy could be the most promising resource for the production of electricity in Maldives. Such resource may include marine current energy, wave energy, and ocean thermal energy conversion (OTEC). Further feasibility studies need to be carried out to determine the real potential and the best technological pathways and costs of these options. A progressive development of sites (phased approach) seems to be an attractive strategy for developers. The base case scenario foresees up to 7 MW in ocean energy projects between 2028 and 2030. The paradigm shift scenario raises this target to 40 MW.

Table 12: Integration of Technology Innovation in the Greater Male' Region

| Year | Project Investment | Capacity (MW) | | Investment Mechanism |
		Base Case	Paradigm Shift	
2026–2030	Floating solar with storage	5.0	30.0	Private - PPA
2028–2030	Ocean energy with storage	7.0	40.0	Private - PPA
	Total	**12.0**	**70.0**	

MW = megawatt, PPA = power purchase agreement.
Source: Asian Development Bank.

4.3 Other Inhabited Islands

The base case scenario for other inhabited islands estimates that by 2030, 10% of energy efficiency is achieved (compared to the business-as-usual situation). The paradigm shift scenario increases this target to 15%. Energy efficiency interventions will result in a reduction of the peak day demand from 116 MW to 105 MW in 2030 in the base case scenario, and to 98 MW in the paradigm shift scenario (Figure 19).

The share of renewable energy in the electricity produced in 2030 is estimated at 39% in the base case scenario and at 48% in the paradigm shift scenario. The electricity produced in 2030 is estimated at 270 GWh from renewable energy versus 428 GWh from diesel in the base case scenario, and 315 GWh from renewable energy versus 339 GWh from diesel in the paradigm shift scenario (Figure 20 and Figure 21). The approximate investments needed in new renewable energy infrastructure, including the costs of distribution grid upgrade and storage, are $230 million in the base case scenario, and $270 million in the paradigm shift scenario.

Achieving these targets will result in a reduction of 117,000 tons of diesel consumption in the base case scenario in 2030, and 138,000 tons of diesel in the paradigm shift scenario. This is equivalent to 54% reduction for the base case scenario and 63% reduction for the paradigm shift scenario, when compared with a business-as-usual situation (Figure 22). The interventions considered for other inhabited islands are described in the next paragraphs.

Figure 19: Forecast of the Aggregated Peak Day Demand in Other Inhabited Islands
(megawatt)

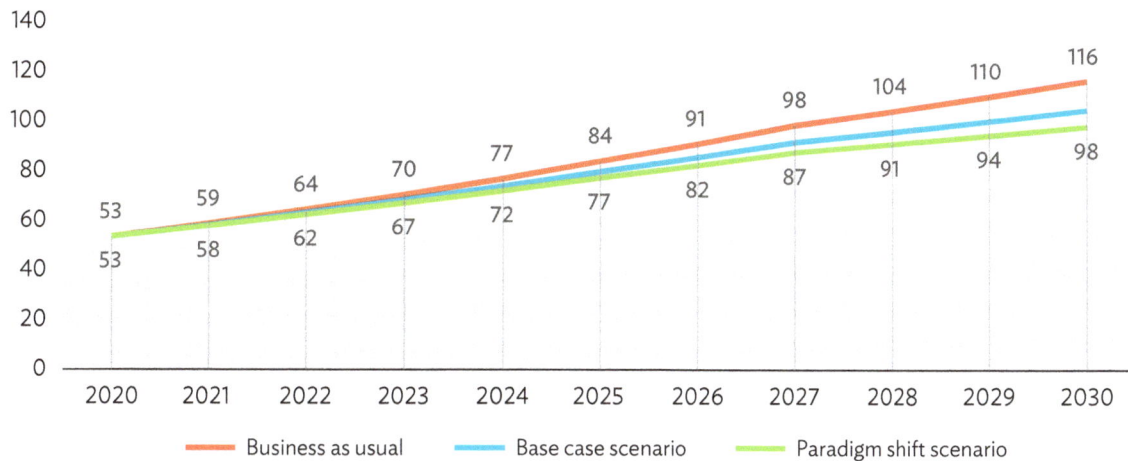

Source: Asian Development Bank.

Figure 20: Forecast of Electricity Production in Other Inhabited Islands—Base Case Scenario
(gigawatt-hour)

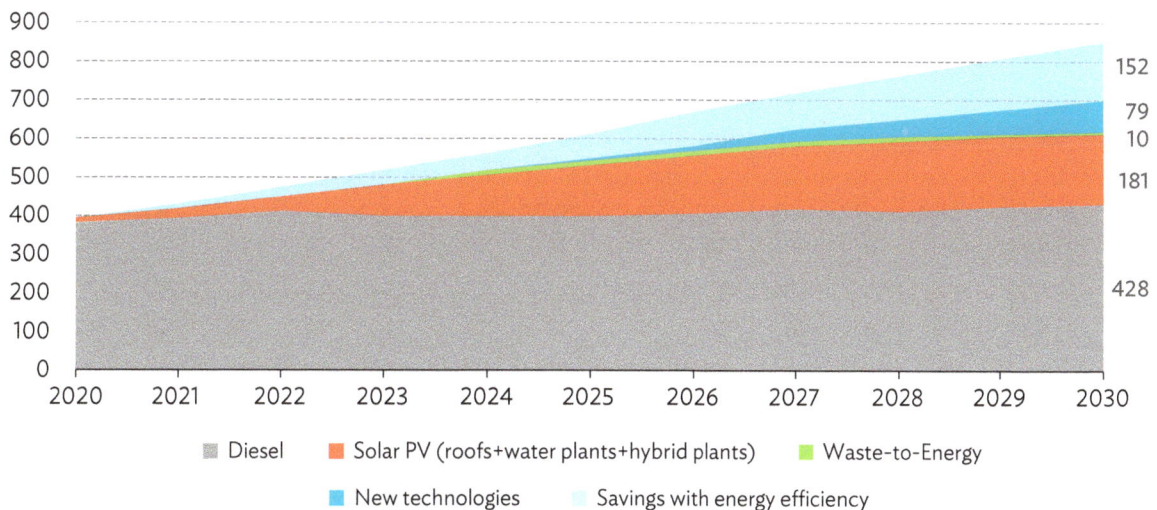

PV = photovoltaic.
Source: Asian Development Bank.

Figure 21: Forecast of Electricity Production in Other Inhabited Islands—Paradigm Shift Scenario
(gigawatt-hour)

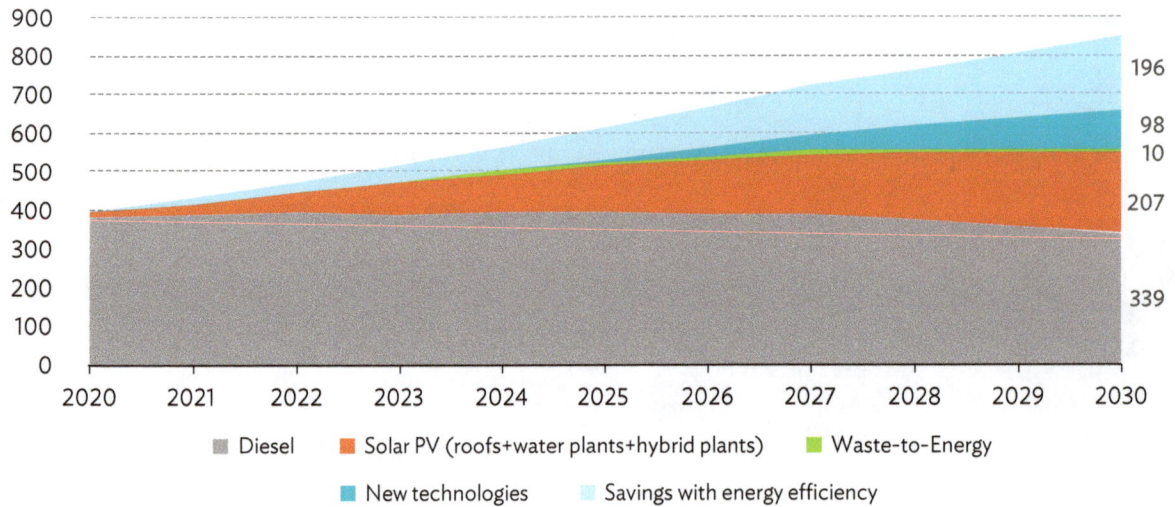

Values at 2030:
- 196
- 98
- 10
- 207
- 339

Legend:
- Diesel
- Solar PV (roofs+water plants+hybrid plants)
- Waste-to-Energy
- New technologies
- Savings with energy efficiency

PV = photovoltaic.
Source: Asian Development Bank.

Figure 22: Forecast of Diesel Use in Electricity Production in Other Inhabited Islands
('000 tons)

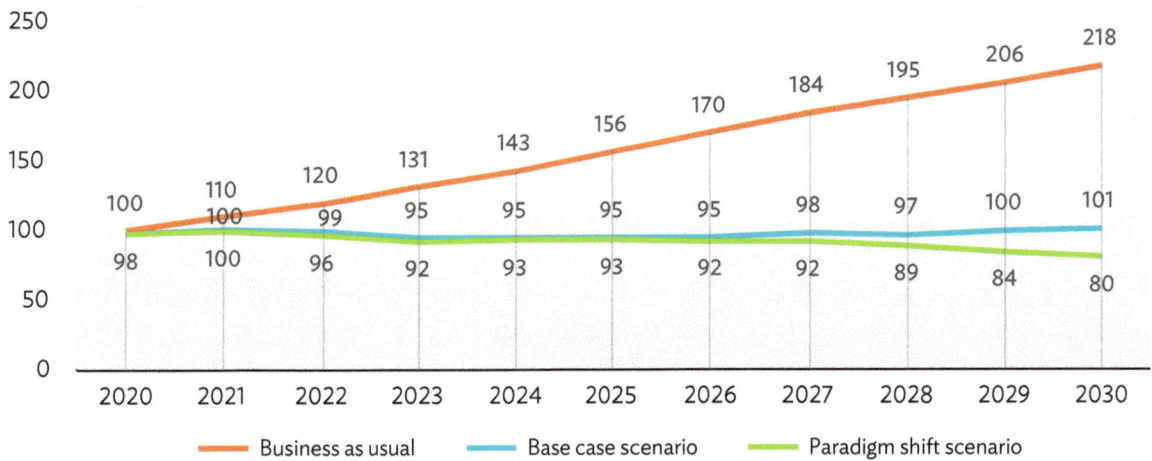

Business as usual: 100, 110, 120, 131, 143, 156, 170, 184, 195, 206, 218

Base case scenario: 100, 100, 99, 95, 95, 95, 95, 98, 97, 100, 101

Paradigm shift scenario: 98, 100, 96, 92, 93, 93, 92, 92, 89, 84, 80

Years: 2020, 2021, 2022, 2023, 2024, 2025, 2026, 2027, 2028, 2029, 2030

Legend:
- Business as usual
- Base case scenario
- Paradigm shift scenario

Source: Asian Development Bank.

Energy Efficiency - Supply Side

1. Interconnection of islands

FENAKA has identified seven cases where distance between islands is smaller than 2 km and interconnection seems possible. Resulting electrical systems would range between 2 MW to 10 MW. Interconnections will be done either with a submarine cable or aerial cable, depending on the depth of the sea and traffic of vessels. Feasibility studies are being carried out.

2. Reduction of distribution losses

The current average distribution loss in other inhabited islands is estimated at 12%. The upgrading of grids aims to reduce this loss to 5% by 2030. Upgrading of distribution grids in other inhabited islands should include smart metering, automation of distribution systems, and remote data acquisition.

Energy Efficiency - Demand Side

1. Efficient lighting

The implementation of a national LED street lighting program is recommended. Regarding indoors lighting, the "FahiAli" program, managed by the Ministry of Environment, illustrates well the success story of the promotion of efficient lighting. Phase 3 of this program has handed a total of 262,500 LED lights to FENAKA Corporation Limited for distribution to each beneficiary household. Previously, phase 2 of this program distributed 75,000 LED lights to different institutions and individuals, and 534 harbor lights were provided to seven islands. Phase 1 of the program distributed a total of 265,000 LED lights to 164 islands and 511 institutions.

2. Efficient domestic appliances

To achieve the energy efficiency target, programs for shifting to efficient air-conditioners, refrigerators, washing machines, and microwaves should be implemented. In the paradigm shift scenario, these interventions are complemented with economic incentives and microcredit programs for the replacement of inefficient lighting and household appliances.

Renewable Energy Infrastructure

The base case scenario foresees the installation of 110.5 MW of renewable energy capacity in other inhabited islands, and the paradigm shift scenario estimates 128.5 MW (Table 13). The larger part of this new infrastructure corresponds to hybrid systems owned by Maldives' utilities, FENAKA, and STELCO. The POISED project will finalize the installation and start of operations of 24.0 MW within the next 2 years.

The rest of the foreseen renewable energy infrastructure is intended as private sector investments. These investments will be secured by either a power purchase agreement (PPA) for the larger infrastructure, or net-metering tariffing for small rooftop installations.

Table 13: Renewable Energy Infrastructure for Other Inhabited Islands, 2020–2030

Year	Project Investment	Capacity (MW) Base Case	Capacity (MW) Paradigm Shift	Investment Mechanism
2020–2023	POISED hybrid plants	24.0	24.0	Public sector – Utilities
2020–2023	Roof top PV Addu and others	4.5	4.5	Private – Net metering
2022–2030	Upgrade of POISED hybrid plants complemented with storage	70.0	83.0	Public sector – Utilities
2024–2026	Waste-to-energy plants	2.0	2.0	Private – PPA
2026–2030	Micro rooftop wind turbines	10.0	15.0	Private – Net metering
	Total	**110.5**	**128.5**	

MW = megawatt, POISED = Preparing Outer Island Sustainable Electricity Development Project, PPA = power purchase agreement, PV = photovoltaic.
Source: Asian Development Bank.

1. Hybrid diesel-photovoltaic power plants

The proposed solution for the rest of inhabited islands is the hybridization of existing power plants with renewable energy, complemented with energy storage systems and governed with an adequate energy management system (EMS). Hybrid system configurations allow all energy sources to supply peak loads from combined sources by synchronizing the inverter and supplying the load separately at medium- or low-load demand. The bidirectional inverter can charge the battery bank when the diesel generator has available surplus of energy and operating as a DC-AC converter (inverter operation) when the diesel generator is switched off.

By 2023, the power plants in all other inhabited islands should be hybridized. By the end of 2020, FENAKA will install, with government funding, 2.8 MWp in 20 hybrid plants of less than 150 kW.

Hybrid systems should be designed to easily scale-up to progressively making renewable energy as the primary source of energy and the diesel generator mainly as backup. And, wherever it is feasible, plans for the construction of water desalination plants should be coupled with existing and future power plants to take advantage of potential synergies. The continuous hybridization of power plants and upgrading of existing hybrid power plants will follow the lessons learned in the POISED project:[19]

- **Raising awareness about the benefits of renewable energy.** Past experiences in Maldives have raised doubts among the public on the benefits of renewable energy. Several agencies (i.e., ADB, JICA, World Bank) have continually worked on renewable energy projects that aim to raise awareness and demonstrate proof of the concept. Dissemination efforts by the POISED project have been relevant to gain public support to hybrid systems.

---

[19] Climate Investment Fund. 2019. Preparing Outer Island Sustainable Electricity Development Project (POISED). *CIF-GDI Delivery Challenge Case Study.*

- **Finding solutions to finance.** Given the country's size and its borrowing constraints, the typical funding mechanisms are small grants or loans. The POISED program has made a sound case for larger funding since it has mobilized nearly $129 million through a concessional combination of grants and loans. The POISED financing scheme has helped develop a program that meaningfully addresses fossil fuel dependence and emission reductions. POISED financing, however, has not been free of problems. One loan of $10 million did not materialize, and another loan of $50 million was put on hold for a period of time. Additional finance from ADB and a grant from the European Union were mobilized to cover the financing gap. The Government of Maldives has adopted all the needed flexibilities in the project design phase to ensure successful implementation.
- **Increasing local training and capacities.** Local knowledge and skills have been difficult to find for some time. Foreign contractors constantly faced problems in the installation and testing of the solar PV-battery-diesel hybrid systems due to the limited technical capacity at local level. POISED has experienced a steep learning curve with foreign and local contractors toward building sufficient capacities to continue the project.

2. Waste-to-energy

Two waste-to-energy (WTE) plants are also suggested for other inhabited islands—one for Addu (1,500 kW) and another one for R. Vandhoo island (500 kW).

3. Rooftop solar PV and rooftop micro wind turbines

Rooftop solar PV installation has already been successful in Addu City. This experience can be replicated in other medium-sized islands. The base case scenario includes achieving the installation of 4.5 MWp rooftop solar PV in Addu and other inhabited islands under the net-metering tariffing system. Rooftop micro wind turbines are also considered in both scenarios, and under the same net-metering tariffing system.

Integration of Technology Innovation

The base case scenario estimates the testing and integration of innovative renewable energy technologies at 18 MW between 2025 and 2030, and the paradigm shift scenario raises this target to 22.5 MW (Table 14). The investment mechanism chosen for these demonstration projects is PPA.

Table 14: Integration of Technology Innovation in Other Inhabited Islands

| Year | Project Investment | Capacity (MW) | | Investment Mechanism |
		Base Case	Paradigm Shift	
2025–2030	Floating PV with storage	15.0	15.0	Private - PPA
2028–2030	Ocean energy with storage	3.0	7.5	Private - PPA
	Total	**18.0**	**22.5**	

MW = megawatt, PPA = power purchase agreement, PV = photovoltaic.
Source: Asian Development Bank.

1. Floating PV and ocean energy pilots

The first pilot projects with floating solar in other inhabited islands have started. A pilot floating solar plant of 150 kWp has been installed in Dharavandhoo island (Baa Atoll). The project owner is already planning to upgrade this small floating PV plant with an addition of 500 kW (resulting in a total of 650 kWp floating solar plant). Both scenarios include the deployment of 15 MWp in floating solar plants after 2025, once technology challenges are known better. The installation of ocean energy infrastructure (with storage) is also considered in both scenarios after 2028.

2. Hydrogen storage and fuel cells technology

Hydrogen fuel cells—having hydrogen produced with renewable energies—are an alternative to decarbonized generators, as well as over conventional lithium-ion battery energy storage systems. Hydrogen is best suited where it has lower cost compared with regular electricity storage batteries. The cost of hydrogen generators is mainly influenced by two factors: the cost of the fuel cell and the tank system, and the cost of hydrogen production and its distribution. The cost of fuel cells and storage tanks are projected to drop up to 70% by 2030. This will be possible due to growing hydrogen volumes in the market, including in transportation. The cost of hydrogen production could drop by up to 60% over the next decade.[20] It is estimated that cost competitiveness of hydrogen storage for Maldives may arrive toward the end of the decade.

The fuel cell system is similar for different applications. Two technologies are mostly used to produce hydrogen from electrolysis, and in combination with renewable electricity—alkaline and proton-exchange membrane (PEM). Alkaline is at present the most mature technology. It uses a saline solution to separate hydrogen from water molecules by applying electricity. PEM uses a solid membrane and an electric charge to separate the hydrogen from water molecules. Fuel cells have longer life and are not affected by tropical temperatures in the same way batteries are (temperature tolerance for fuel cells is from -40°C to 55°C). Fuel cells occupy up to 10 times less space for the same capacity, and they require lower maintenance (one to two inspections per year compared with frequent maintenance needed by batteries). Pilot projects are needed to determine which option is the most economically viable for Maldives.

4.4 Resorts, Industrial, and Agricultural Islands

Maldives is a leading destination for high-end tourism. Tourism is the largest economic activity, earning foreign exchange revenues and generating employment all over the country. Maldives has 145 islands and marinas exclusively dedicated to resorts. All tourist resort islands have their own private electricity production through diesel generators. During the first semester of 2019, international flights expanded by a record 18.2% compared to 2018. Hotels and resorts expanded their bed capacity by 10.9% in the same period. Overall, tourism earnings, measured by bed-nights occupancy, grew by 14.7% in the first semester of 2019.[21] The unexpected and massive economic

---

20   Hydrogen Council. 2020. *Path to Hydrogen Competitiveness: A Cost Perspective*. Brussels.
21   ADB. 2019. *Maldives Economic Update 2019*. Manila.

crisis caused by the COVID-19 pandemic has disrupted all plans in the tourism industry, and practically put it at a standstill since March 2020. Economic recovery of the sector will depend on how fast the tourism flows regain momentum over the next years. The country's "one-island, one-resort" approach will facilitate the implementation of social distancing measures in resorts, which is expected to strengthen the sector's ability to recover sooner.

Fisheries and agriculture are the leading production activities of the country. Compared to 2017, the end of 2018 has recorded a 5.5% growth in fish catch (footnote 2). Fisheries has also been impacted by the pandemic. Exports of fresh, chilled, or frozen tuna accounted for 70% of all domestic goods exports over the past years. Only in March 2020 has tuna exports fallen by 60%. This was mainly due to logistics difficulties in transporting shipments to Thailand and the closing down of borders by the European Union, with subsequent stopping of all international flights traveling to and from Maldives. After the European markets began to reopen in mid-May 2020, the sector showed its first signs of recovery.[22] The fishery industry will have to make efforts to develop fish products with high value added addressed to premium markets. This will require policy attention intended to increase productivity and quality. The capacity of Maldives Industrial Fisheries Company should be expanded as well. Additional financing under the POISED project will also consider the installation of ice-making factories powered with renewable energy. These investments aim to increase the resilience of fisheries activities in the inhabited islands. The government will also explore the potential of mariculture, aquaculture, and reef fishing (footnote 21).

In relation to agriculture, there were 7,568 farmers in 2018. The highest number of farmers are found at Laamu atoll (22.6% of the total farmers). By the end of 2018, six islands were leased for agricultural purposes (footnote 1). Due to the pandemic crisis, Maldives has no other choice but to increase its agricultural production yields and variety by incorporating modern climate-smart practices that will require reliable energy supply. Farming in Maldives is in need of rapid transformation to reach targets of food imports substitution.[23]

The base case scenario for resorts, industrial, and agricultural islands estimates that by 2030, 10% of energy efficiency is achieved (compared to the business-as-usual situation). The paradigm shift scenario increases this target to 20%. Energy efficiency interventions will result in a reduction of the aggregated peak day demand from 186 MW to 167 MW in 2030 in the base case scenario, and to 149 MW in the paradigm shift scenario (Figure 23).

---

[22] World Bank Group. 2020b. *Maldives Development Update: In Stormy Seas*. Washington, DC.
[23] Statement by the Minister of Fisheries, Marine Resources and Agriculture at the signing ceremony of the Sustainable Economic Empowerment and Development for SMEs project to provide economic rehabilitation amidst COVID-19, supported by the Government of Japan. 11 June 2020.

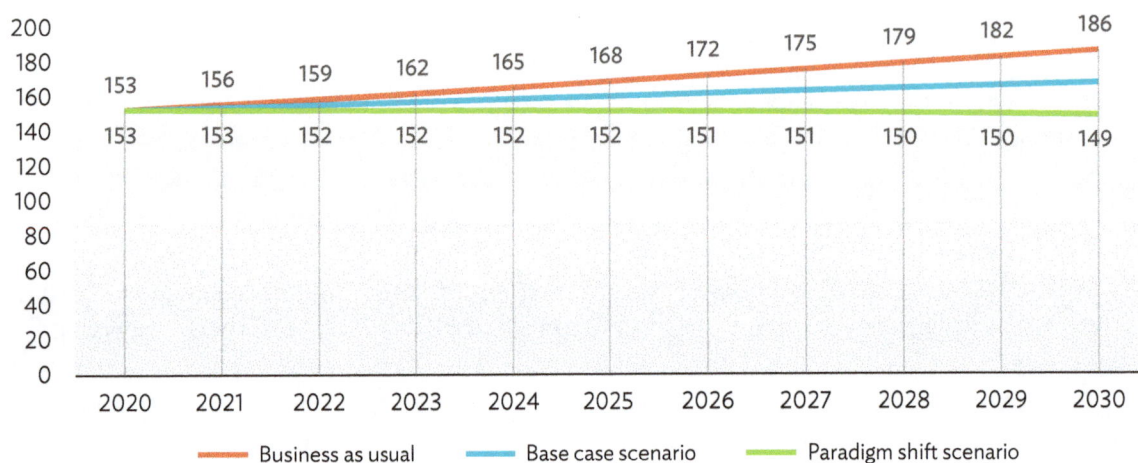

Figure 23: Forecast for the Aggregated Peak Day Demand In Resorts, Industrial, and Agricultural Islands
(megawatt)

Business as usual: 153, 156, 159, 162, 165, 168, 172, 175, 179, 182, 186

Paradigm shift scenario: 153, 153, 152, 152, 152, 152, 151, 151, 150, 150, 149

2020 2021 2022 2023 2024 2025 2026 2027 2028 2029 2030

Business as usual — Base case scenario — Paradigm shift scenario

Source: Asian Development Bank.

The share of renewable energy in the electricity produced in 2030 is estimated at 15% in the base case scenario and at 50% in the paradigm shift scenario The electricity produced in 2030 is estimated at 103 GWh from renewable energy versus 591 GWh from diesel in the base case scenario, and 311 GWh from renewable energy versus 306 GWh from diesel in the paradigm shift scenario (Figure 24 and Figure 25). The approximate investments needed in new renewable energy infrastructure, storage and grid upgrading are $230 million in the best case scenario, and $680 million in the paradigm shift scenario.

Achieving these targets will result in a reduction of 48,000 tons of diesel consumption in the base case scenario in 2030, and 115,000 tons of diesel in the paradigm shift scenario. This is equivalent to 26% reduction for the base case scenario and 62% reduction for the paradigm shift scenario, when compared with a business-as-usual situation (Figure 26). This will require a policy direction for resorts to promote the conversion of their diesel generators to hybrid or full renewable energy systems; otherwise, they will be subject to additional diesel taxes. The interventions considered for resorts, industrial, and agricultural islands are described in the next paragraphs.

Figure 24: Forecast of the Electricity Production in Resorts, Industrial, and Agricultural Islands—Base Case Scenario
(gigawatt-hour)

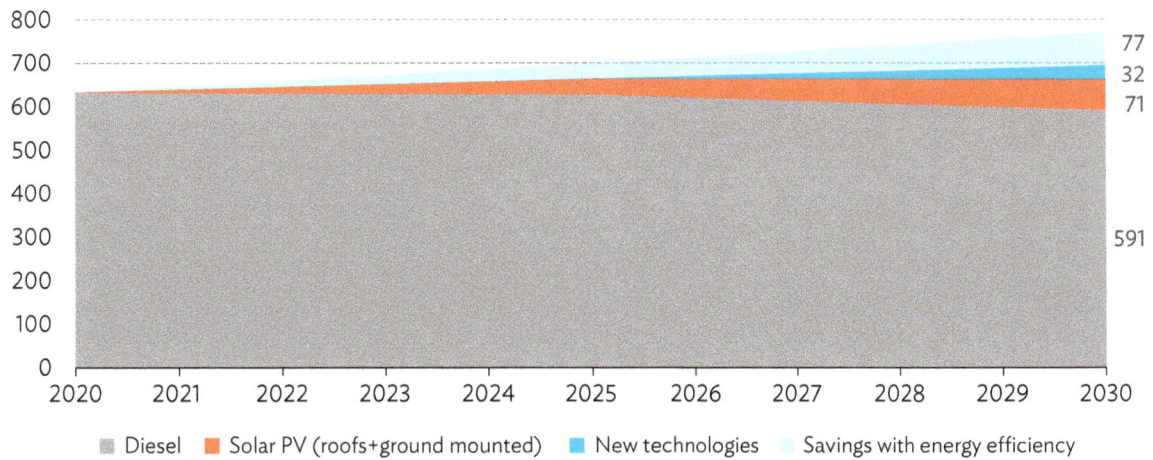

Diesel   Solar PV (roofs+ground mounted)   New technologies   Savings with energy efficiency

PV = photovoltaic.
Source: Asian Development Bank.

Figure 25: Forecast of the Electricity Production in Resorts, Industrial, and Agricultural Islands—Paradigm Shift Scenario
(gigawatt-hour)

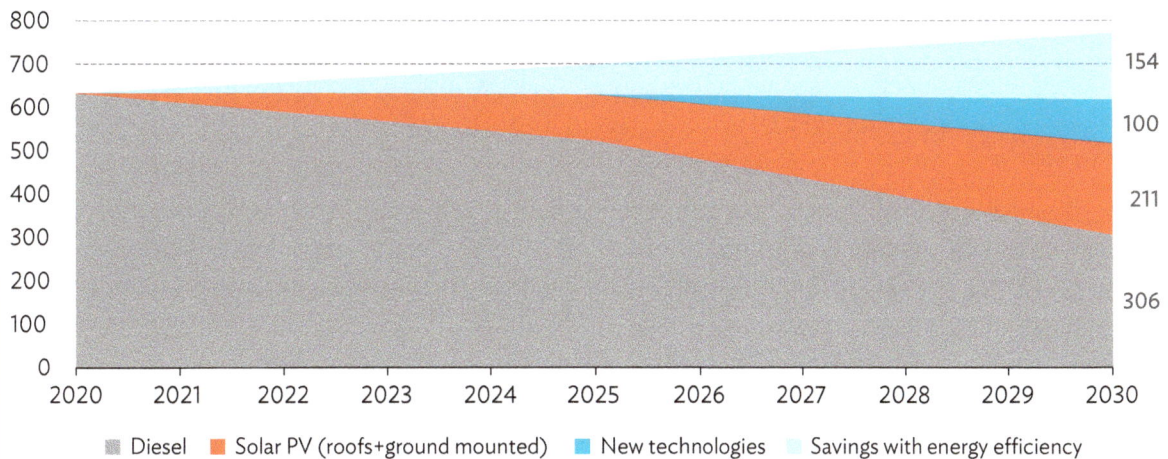

Diesel   Solar PV (roofs+ground mounted)   New technologies   Savings with energy efficiency

PV = photovoltaic.
Source: Asian Development Bank.

Figure 26: Forecast of Diesel Use in Electricity Production in Resorts, Industrial, and Agricultural Islands
('000 tons)

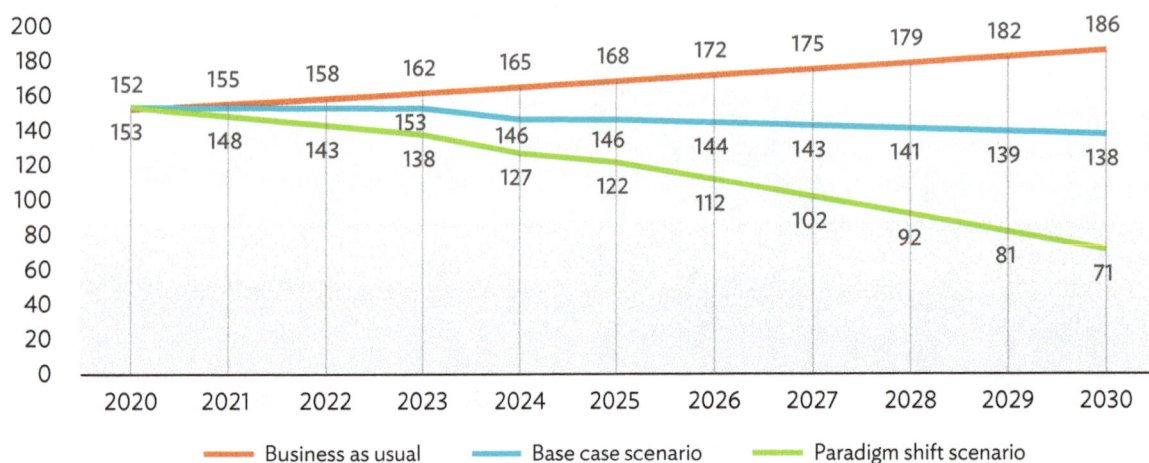

Business as usual — Base case scenario — Paradigm shift scenario

Source: Asian Development Bank.

Energy Efficiency in Resort Islands

Electricity consumption in resorts can be breakdown into—40% for air-conditioning, 10% for refrigerators, 10% for desalination plants, 10% for lighting, and 20% for laundry services.[24] This means that more than 60% of the energy consumption in resorts is due to energy use of appliances and building types. Policies on appliances and labeling can significantly help save energy in resorts. Interventions proposed are as follows:

1. Energy audits and plans for continuous improvement

- **Mapping resorts.** To quantify the potential for energy efficiency through an inventory of energy consumption and equipment used.
- **Energy efficiency audits.** These audits should identify the most viable options for energy savings and should lead to the establishment of energy management and accounting centers in each resort. Audits are useful to benchmark energy performance against international best practices, other resorts in Maldives, and the country's own historical data.
- **Energy efficiency plans.** With targets based on a resort's room capacity, including at least the following measures:
    - find the optimal curve for fuel consumption for electricity production vs. load test (efficiency);
    - insulate high temperature surfaces of generator set exhaust systems;
    - install individual diesel flow meters for each diesel generator;

---

[24] BeCitizen. 2010. *Maldives 2009 Carbon Audit Report*. Paris.

- o operate the diesel generators within their sustainable power (load) range;
- o develop preventive maintenance programs for air-conditioners;
- o replace old air-conditioners with new ones rated at and with energy efficiency ratio (EER) 12 British thermal units per watt-hour (Btu/Wh) or above; and
- o install air-conditioners condensate collection system.

2. Energy conservation

- **Energy efficiency labeling in appliances.** In particular for air-conditioners, refrigerators, washing machines, microwaves, and electrical and induction stoves.
- **Renewable cooling.** Promote the introduction of solar water heating (SWH), seawater air-conditioning (SWAC), and solar air-conditioning (SAC) technologies. These technologies reduce the electricity demand for heating and cooling, and they also contribute to a larger share of renewable energy. SWH is an excellent option for resorts. It is a mature technology which has demonstrated that it can lower the cost of water heating. Dedicated feasibility studies are required for SWAC and SAC to confirm whether these systems can deliver cost-competitive air-conditioning services. They are dependent on the techno-economic accessibility to deep waters. These technologies usually require a large cooling load to be economically feasible.

The successful implementation of the above measures requires Maldives to explore and propose incentives to resorts, and a mechanism to monitor and verify the incentives claims. This Road Map proposes the establishment of a "**zero fossil fuel energy**" label and program. The government should use the label of this program to actively promote sustainable tourism in associated resorts. Any financial incentive (such as duty exemptions) should be reserved only for associated resorts.

Energy Efficiency in Industrial and Agricultural Islands

Energy efficiency in all industrial islands are crucial for achieving the Road Map targets. Energy efficiency actions addressed to large-scale cooling related to the fishing industry should be carefully designed. Fish and fisheries products require substantial cooling to ensure products are maintained at exceptional quality. These plans and actions should not focus only on cooling systems installed on islands, but also on those refrigeration systems installed on board fishing vessels. It is anticipated that more than 150 to 200 fishing vessels will be fitted with such systems by 2023.[25] Actions toward achieving an optimal energy efficiency in industrial and agricultural islands include the following:

1. Energy audits and plans for continuous improvement

- **Mapping of industries.** Categorize different industries and develop a data reporting mechanism for industrial and agricultural islands.

---

[25] Government of Maldives, Ministry of Fisheries, Marine Resources and Agriculture.

- **Energy audits.** Energy audits could be made mandatory for industries with loads of more than 100 kW. Results are useful to benchmark performance.
- **Digitalization of processes.** Energy efficiency programs can introduce low-cost sensors to monitor and control processes on industrial and agricultural islands.

2. Energy conservation

- **Use of waste-heat recovery.** Exhaust gases from diesel generators can be used in different applications including air-conditioners of public buildings through vapor absorption machines (VAM), and for ice-making industries.
- **Technical standards for imported equipment.** Develop and promote minimum standards for equipment imported into the country, in particular, electrical motors, water pumps, and air-conditioning units.
- **Renewable cooling.** Promote seawater air-conditioning (SWAC) systems for large users. Implementation of a program to monitor improvements and channel incentives to operators of industrial islands awarded for fisheries projects, other industrial activities, and agricultural islands is recommended.

Renewable Energy Infrastructure and Integration of Technology Innovation

The base case scenario proposes the target of 50 MWp in PV installations to be installed in resorts, industrial, and agricultural islands by 2030. The paradigm shift scenario establishes this target at 150 MWp. Following the experiences in the rest of the country, it is also proposed that a 16 MWp of floating solar are installed in the base case scenario in these islands after 2026, and 50 MWp in the paradigm shift scenario (Table 15).

Table 15: Proposed Project Investments in Resorts, Industrial, and Agricultural Islands

Year	Project Investment	Capacity (MWp)		Investment Mechanism
		Base Case	Paradigm Shift	
2020–2030	PV installations	50.0	150.0	Private sector
2024–2030	Floating PV with storage	16.0	50.0	Private sector
	Total	**66.0**	**200.0**	

MWp = megawatt-peak, PV = photovoltaic.
Source: Asian Development Bank.

4.5 Resulting Country Energy Matrix

The aggregate results at country level are shown in Figures 27, 28, and 29.

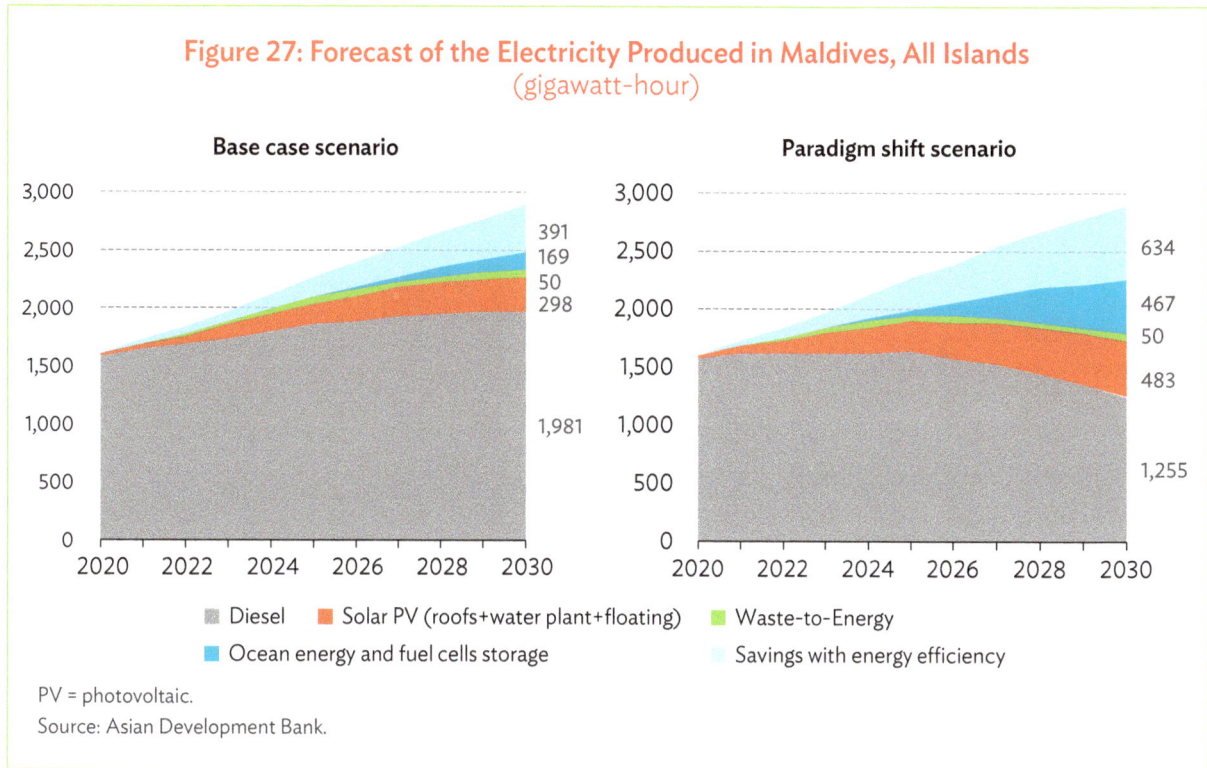

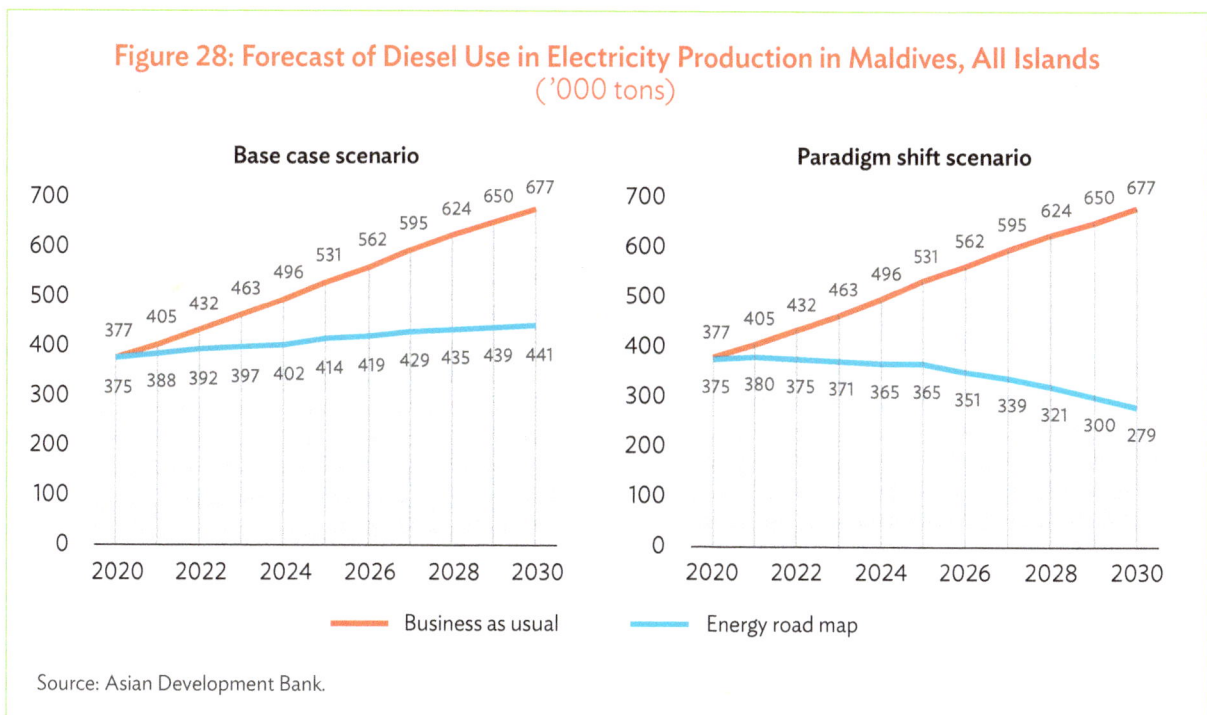

Figure 27: Forecast of the Electricity Produced in Maldives, All Islands
(gigawatt-hour)

Base case scenario

Value
391
169
50
298
1,981

Paradigm shift scenario

Value
634
467
50
483
1,255

Legend:
- Diesel
- Solar PV (roofs+water plant+floating)
- Waste-to-Energy
- Ocean energy and fuel cells storage
- Savings with energy efficiency

PV = photovoltaic.
Source: Asian Development Bank.

Figure 28: Forecast of Diesel Use in Electricity Production in Maldives, All Islands
('000 tons)

Base case scenario

Business as usual: 377, 405, 432, 463, 496, 531, 562, 595, 624, 650, 677
Energy road map: 375, 388, 392, 397, 402, 414, 419, 429, 435, 439, 441

Paradigm shift scenario

Business as usual: 377, 405, 432, 463, 496, 531, 562, 595, 624, 650, 677
Energy road map: 375, 380, 375, 371, 365, 365, 351, 339, 321, 300, 279

Legend:
- Business as usual
- Energy road map

Source: Asian Development Bank.

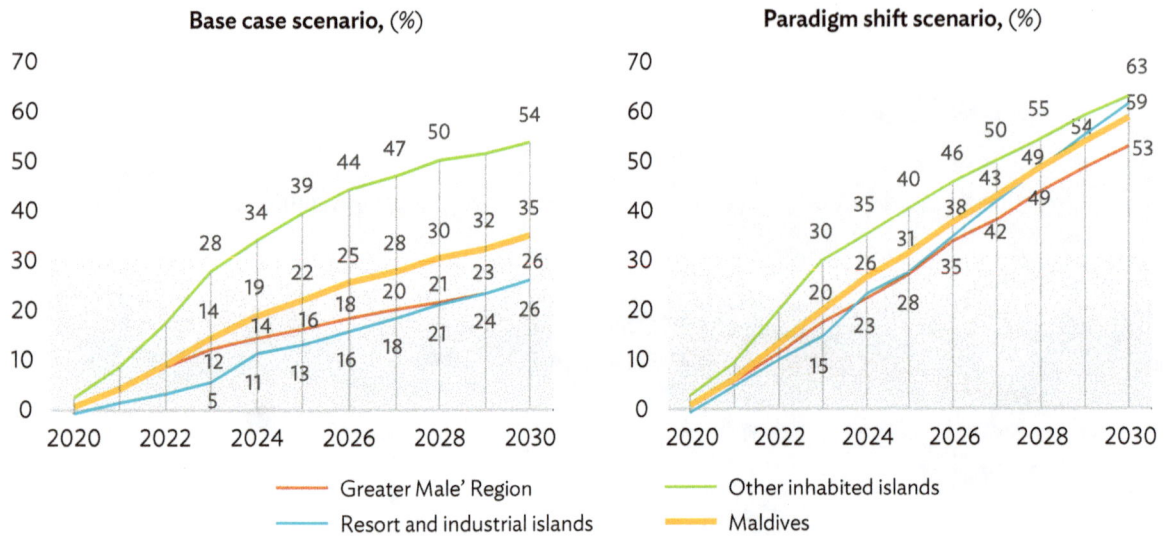

Figure 29: Forecast of the Reduction in Diesel Use for Electricity Production in Maldives, All Islands

Source: Asian Development Bank.

5 STRATEGY FOR OTHER SUBSECTORS

5.1   Flagship Interventions

The energy used in the sea transport, road transport, and cooking subsectors are also covered by this Road Map. Interventions in energy efficiency, demand curtail, fuel substitution, and integration of technology innovation are foreseen. Flagship interventions for these three subsectors are listed in Table 16.

Table 16: Road Map Interventions for the Electricity Subsector

Energy Efficiency	Demand Curtail	Fuel Substitution	Integration of Technology Innovation
Replacement of inefficient vessels and boats	Reduction of vehicle registration and promotion of public transportation	Promotion of electric buses, vehicles, and bikes	Introduction of hybrid solar boats
Replacement of inefficient vessels and boats		Natural gas as alternative fuel for large vessels, buses, and vehicles	Feasibility and piloting of hydrogen fueled vessels
		Replacement of LPG stoves with electric induction stoves	

LPG = liquefied petroleum gas.
Source: Asian Development Bank.

The design and monitoring framework for the base case and paradigm shift scenarios for the sea transport, road transport, and cooking subsectors are presented in Appendixes 3 and 4 of this report. The following sections detail these interventions.

5.2 Sea Transport

The 2030 target for diesel consumption reduction in the sea transport subsector is 22% in the base case scenario and 42% in the paradigm shift scenario, compared to business as usual (Figure 30). Specific measures proposed are as follows:

- **Replacement of inefficient fleet.** Replace existing vessels with more efficient units with the support of a government incentives program. This program should aim to improve the average specific consumption of vessels by 20% in the base case scenario, and by 40% in the paradigm shift scenario.
- **Hybrid solar boats.** Introduce hybrid solar boats for short-distance travel, particularly for tourism purposes. The aim is to achieve a 2.5% share of hybrid solar boats by 2030 in both scenarios. Electric motors in hybrid boats run on batteries charged with power supplied by solar panels mounted on the boat. Hybrid solar boats have the advantage of no sound and vibrations and fuel odor free when propelled by the electric motor.
- **Natural gas as alternative fuel for large vessels.** Large vessels exclusively running on LNG or that have dual fuel engines are growing in number and are an option for tankers, container vessels, and cruises. The future international cargo port in Gulhifalhu could have a filling station in case the installation of small-scale LNG infrastructure in the Greater Male' Region is decided. A specific feasibility study is required to assess the benefits and costs of this proposed measure.

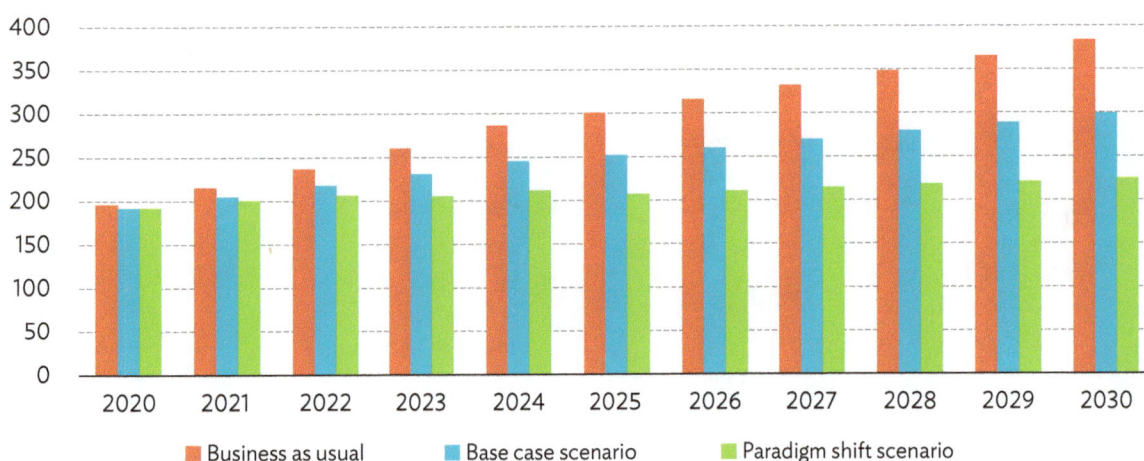

Figure 30: Forecast of Diesel Use in Sea Transport Compared to Business as Usual
('000 tons)

Source: Asian Development Bank.

- **Feasibility and piloting of hydrogen-fueled vessels.** A hydrogen-fueled vessel can either have an internal combustion engine or an electric motor. Internal combustion engines use hydrogen fuel. Electrical motors are powered by a fuel cell. A complete feasibility study and pilot test are needed to assess the benefits and costs of transforming jetties into using hydrogen fuel and installing small mobile hydrogen stations on islands that can store hydrogen produced by excess renewable energy.

5.3   Road Transport

The 2030 target for petrol consumption reduction in the road transport subsector is 22% in the base case scenario and 52% in the paradigm shift scenario, compared to business as usual (Figure 31). Specific measures proposed are described in the next paragraphs.

- **Replacement of inefficient fleet.** Replace existing vehicles and motorbikes with more efficient units, including hybrid vehicles, with the support of a government incentives program. The aim of this program is that the average specific consumption of vehicles improves by 20% in the base case scenario, and by 40% in the paradigm shift scenario.
- **Electric buses, vehicles, and motorbikes.** Introduce full electric buses, vehicles, and motorbikes nationwide. The aim is to achieve a 2.5% share of electric units by 2030 in the base case scenario and 20% in the paradigm shift scenario. Electric vehicles require proper charging infrastructure, which requires an important transformational change in transport policies.
- **Reduction of vehicles registration.** The global trend is to move from the use of personal vehicles to efficient and sustainable public transportation. This trend may be facilitated by placing restrictions on the issuance of new registrations or putting restrictions on the age of vehicles allowed on the roads.

Figure 31: Forecast of Petrol Use in Road Transport Compared to Business as Usual
(´000 tons)

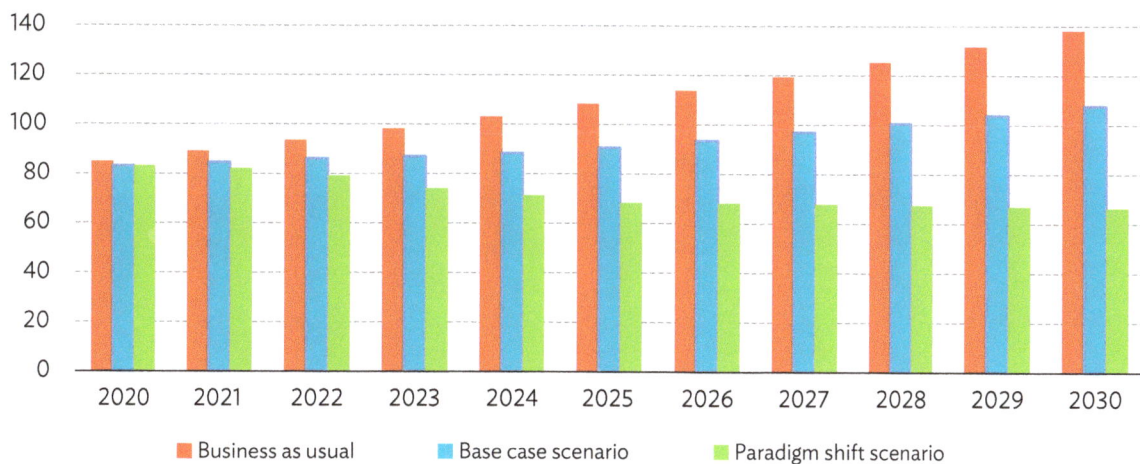

Source: Asian Development Bank.

- **Natural gas as alternative fuel for vehicles.** Natural-gas-fueled vehicles emit 20% to 29% less CO_2 than vehicles fueled with diesel or petrol. Emissions from natural gas are cleaner than diesel, and this alternative fuel produces lower particulate emissions per equivalent distance traveled. A feasibility study is required to assess the benefits and costs of introducing natural-gas-fueled vehicles in the Greater Male' Region where fueling stations could be established in case the installation of small-scale LNG infrastructure in the Greater Male' Region is decided on.

5.4 Liquefied Petroleum Gas Use in Cooking

The 2030 target for the reduction of LPG use in cooking is 35% in the base case scenario and 50% in the paradigm shift scenario, compared to business as usual (Figure 32). This is achieved by establishing an awareness campaign, promoting microcredit programs to replace conventional stoves using bottled LPG with efficient and modern (electric) induction stoves, and reducing or removing subsidies to LPG used in cooking.

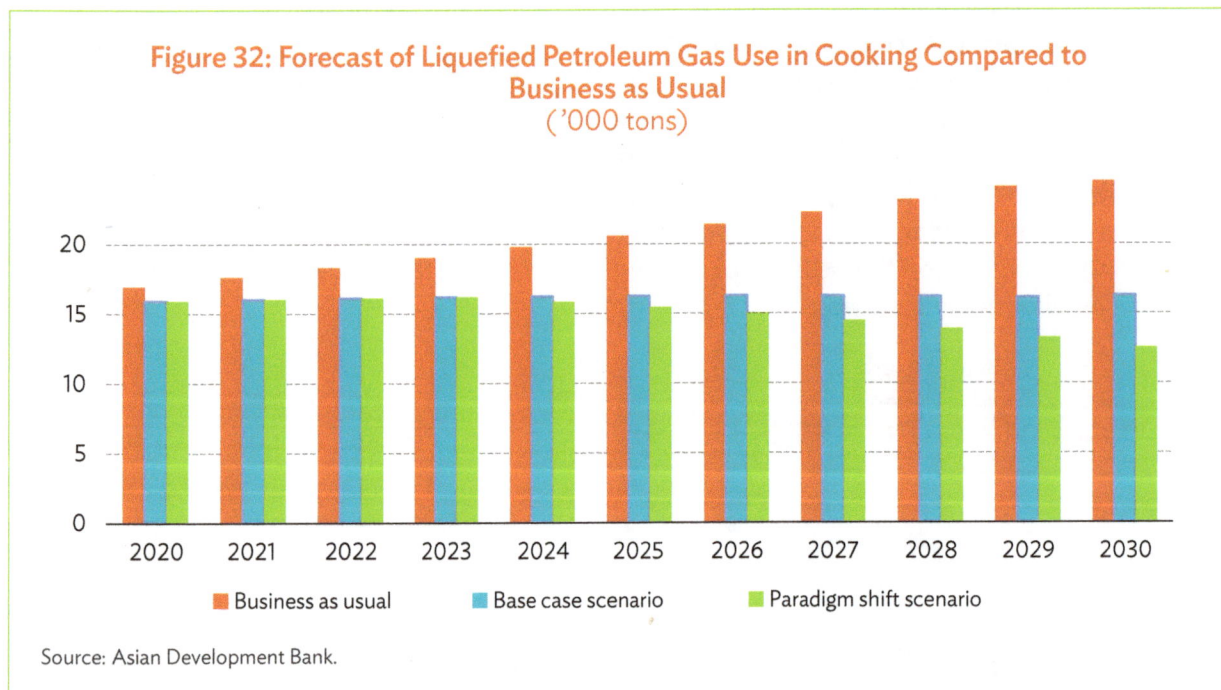

Figure 32: Forecast of Liquefied Petroleum Gas Use in Cooking Compared to Business as Usual
('000 tons)

Source: Asian Development Bank.

6 ENABLING THE TRANSITION

Going from a fossil-fuel-based energy sector to a brighter future powered by renewables is a capital-intensive commitment, especially for the islands. Private sector participation is crucial for achieving a low-carbon energy sector. However, attracting private sector participation in Maldives' energy sector has proven to be a complex challenge. Private sector participation can result in the creation of new jobs. Policies should be established to engage local SMEs for the installation and maintenance of renewable energy infrastructure. Such a measure is highly relevant as it facilitates the creation of new business models that can help mitigate the effects of the crisis from COVID-19 pandemic. Subsidies to fossil fuels and electricity could also be phased out, or rather, directed specifically to the most vulnerable end users that need them. An enabling environment to facilitate this transition is needed for the successful implementation of the energy road map. The Government of Maldives should provide such enabling environment to confer authority, build consensus, attract attention to, and provide resources for the road map implementation.

6.1 Policy and Regulatory Measures

The regulatory framework should constantly be revised and adapted to technical developments and economic challenges. Table 17 lists the proposed regulatory measures.

Electricity—Supply Side

1. Continuously revise the tariff system

The tariff system should reflect the complexity of deploying and operating renewable energies in the singular context of Maldives. The largest power generation projects could be realized under an auctioning system coupled with the guidelines on power purchase agreements (PPAs). Smaller power generation projects based on renewable energies, such as home systems (rooftop solar or rooftop wind) or drinking water plants, could use a net metering system.

- **Power purchase agreements.** Private sector participation usually takes place through independent power producer (IPP) schemes with a long-term power purchase agreement. The PPA strategy should be carefully designed to be fair with project developers, at the same

Table 17: Policy and Regulatory Measures to Enable Energy Sector Transition

Electricity Supply	Electricity Demand	Sea and Road Transport	LPG Use in Cooking
• Continuous revision of the tariff system • Technical codes and standards • "Zero fossil fuel" program to reward private sector investments	• Building construction code and certification scheme • Energy labeling and support scheme for the replacement of appliances • Regulation for a more collaborative future with consumers	• Phase out vessels, vehicles, and motorbikes with high GHG emissions • Program for the replacement of low-energy efficiency vessels • Program for the replacement of low-energy efficiency vehicles and motorbikes • Promote sustainable public transportation and reduce the number of vehicles	• Program for the replacement of LPG stoves with electrical induction stoves

GHG = greenhouse gas, LPG = liquefied petroleum gas.
Source: Asian Development Bank.

time achieving the maximum benefit for Maldives' consumers. Developers and contractors may perceive payments under PPAs as high risk even when the government provides payment guarantees. Conducting transparent assessments on the impact of investments made by the utilities versus investments made by IPPs is important to adequately estimate investment risks. The continuous revision of PPA guidelines, in the context of the country's wider contractual framework, and to adapt them to current economic and technology status, will facilitate the timely achievement of target investments.

• **Net metering.** Under net metering, electricity can flow in both directions via a bidirectional meter. Active energy consumers can sell the excess electricity they produce to the grid at a reasonable rate or at the avoided cost of supply from the utility. With net metering, residential and business prosumers[26] can either import an equal amount of electricity from the grid as the amount indicated, or, receive a compensation for the net amount of exported electricity at the end of the agreed or regulated settlement period. The net energy recorded on the meter is used to calculate the prosumer's bill. If the amount of electricity consumed from the grid is higher than the amount of electricity supplied to the grid, the prosumer must pay the bill for net electricity consumption. On the other hand, if the amount of electricity exported to the grid is higher than the amount supplied by the grid, then the utility shall allow a credit, in terms

---

[26]   Active consumers are often called "prosumers" because they both consume and produce electricity.

of kWh, which will be rolled over to the next billing period. The rate at which the prosumer is billed is usually regulated and determined considering several factors, such as the consumer tariff type, renewable energy used to produce electricity, installed capacity, and grid network export limitations. In a net metering scheme, the prosumer always abides by the technical requirements and safety regulations set by the corresponding authority. Grid connection is not supposed to be an extra financial burden to prosumers. Costs of connection (other than meters), ancillary services, and security management of the distribution grid should not be transferred to prosumers.

2. Develop technical codes and standards

Developing technical operation codes and technical standards for the equipment used in power generation is also a crucial measure toward enabling energy sector transition.

- **Technical codes for the operation of hybrid power plants.** With increased deployment of renewable energy, particularly solar PV panels in hybrid diesel-PV plants, the basic controller functions should be clearly defined in technical codes. These functions include automatic start-up, shutdown, load sharing, and automatic recovery.
- **Technical standards for equipment.** Standards establishing technical specifications for electricity generation equipment (PV panels, inverters, storage equipment) should be developed and enforced. Compliance with technical standards should be made obligatory in all purchases with public finance.
- **Technical codes for the connection of renewable energy prosumers' systems.** Clearer regulations and technical codes establishing the conditions for the connection to the grids of prosumers' systems are needed. Connection codes ensure proper handling of intermittent energy and ensure grid security.
- **Technical codes for energy storage and ancillary systems.** The management of intermittent electricity supply is greatly enhanced with energy storage. Energy storage also plays an important role as backup solution in processes that need uninterrupted power supply (e.g., medical centers, refrigeration of fish and food provisions). Energy storage can defer investments, such as on new peak diesel power generation capacity or upgrading of distribution electricity grids. Energy storage also facilitates arbitrage opportunities. Arbitrage refers to the storing of energy during low demand periods and high renewable energy supply, so that the stored energy is made available during high demand periods. Energy storage can also deliver power as ancillary services with durations that can last from a fraction of a second to minutes. Technical codes for energy storage and the provision of ancillary services should involve:
  - o   frequency regulation;
  - o   load following, which is similar to frequency regulation, but covers a longer period of time (e.g., 15 minutes to 24 hours);
  - o   voltage support to transmission and distribution grids;
  - o   black start capability for the restart of generation units after system collapse;
  - o   online spinning reserve to compensate unforeseen fluctuations in demand or supply, which should be ready to use in less than 10 minutes; and
  - o   nonspinning reserve (offline) that can be activated quickly and maintained for hours.

3. Develop a "zero fossil fuel" program to channel incentives to private sector investments

Energy transition in resorts and in other privately managed islands is a challenge that requires explicit policy direction coupled with incentives for creative mechanisms that promote change. This Road Map proposes to create a "zero fossil fuel" label and program to channel government incentives, such as preferential taxation, to privately managed islands.

Government incentives should be given against a clear compromise for reducing the consumption of fossil fuels. Resorts and other privately managed islands could apply to the proposed program by submitting their "zero fossil fuel" plans. These plans should include investments in renewable energy, and in case of resorts, industrial, and agricultural islands—energy efficiency actions to reduce their energy consumption.

Preferential taxation, tax reductions or exemptions, or accelerated depreciation are the proposed incentives for this program to mitigate the effects of high capital costs of renewable energy equipment and more efficient appliances. The proposed tax incentives that could be given to program participants are as follows:

- **Reduction of, or exemption from customs duties and value-added tax (VAT).**
  A reduction of, or exemption from levies on imported renewable energy equipment and selected energy-efficient appliances, and the reduction of, or exemption from VAT on such equipment and appliances could be established and extended for a period of 10 years until the end of the Road Map.
- **Green investment tax allowance for assets and projects.** For companies that purchase approved renewable energy equipment and undertake green technology projects for business purposes, such as in resorts, industrial, and agricultural islands.
- **Green income tax exemption**. For companies adopting innovative technologies approved by the government.

For the specific case of resorts, the approved participants will also receive from the government the "zero fossil fuel" label. The Government of Maldives, through its Ministry of Tourism, could actively promote sustainable tourism in such resorts.

Electricity—Demand Side

1. Revise the building construction code and establish a certification scheme for buildings

Maldives' building construction code should be aligned with the vision of the energy sector. Building codes should explicitly require energy efficiency and conservation measures and promote the installation of renewable energy technologies in all new and refurbished buildings. Renewable energy technologies mounted on buildings should include solar thermal water heating, rooftop solar panels, and rooftop micro wind turbines. The building code should provide guidelines for these installations, and potentially, obligations to install them in new buildings—similar to the building construction codes in many developed countries. A certification mechanism to establish the energy efficiency level of buildings should also be implemented. Such certification mechanism will help the government to better leverage on its financial support.

2. Develop energy labeling and support scheme for the replacement of low-energy efficiency appliances

Energy labeling will help citizens and businesses make more informed purchases of appliances, such as air-conditioners, refrigerators, washing machines, electrical induction stoves, TV, and lighting equipment. In parallel, a microfinancial support mechanism for households to replace low-energy efficiency appliances should be developed and implemented. Procurement rules for making mandatory the purchase of energy-efficient appliances by public institutions should also be developed.

3. Develop regulation for a more collaborative future with consumers

Smart technologies will simplify consumers' involvement in the energy market of the future. Integrated automated solutions, smart metering, and smart appliances will revolutionize the management of consumption. These technologies will also facilitate the introduction of electric vehicles. Optimizing the charging and discharging scheduling of electric vehicles can smooth out the real-time power fluctuations of the grid. New business models are being created with the use of all these innovations. Opportunities are created for energy services companies, aggregators, brokers, and data handling companies. This Road Map recommends that studies are carried out to develop future regulation, including vehicle-to-grid (V2G) regulation to prepare and empower consumers for the challenges of the energy market of the future.

Sea and Road Transport

1. Develop regulation and technical standards to phase out vessels, vehicles, and motorbikes with high GHG emissions

Establish regulation and technical standards to limit permitted carbon dioxide (CO_2), nitrogen oxide (NO_x), and sulfur oxide (SO_x) emissions in vessels, buses, vehicles, and motorbikes operating in Maldives. Regulation should aim at phasing out noncompliant vessels and vehicles within a period of 5 years. Regulation must make sure that noncompliant vessels and vehicles no longer operate in Maldives.

2. Establish a program to replace low-energy efficiency vessels

Sea transport is critical to boosting Maldives' development and trade productivity. Reducing the diesel fuel consumption in sea transport without restricting transport activities requires more energy-efficient fleets and more energy-efficient and modern harbor facilities. It is proposed for the government to establish a program that incentivizes the replacement of old and excessively contaminating vessel engines with energy-efficient and modern ones. Incentives can be in the form of duty exemptions, purchase direct subsidy, and/or purchase financing. This program has to make sure that old engines are effectively discarded, and they are not resold in the market. The purchase of hybrid vessels operating partly or fully with renewable energies should be awarded with larger incentives than efficient diesel-only vessels.

3. Establish a program to replace low-energy efficiency vehicles and motorbikes

The main mitigation action in the road transport sector is related with the number of operating units and their efficiency. It is proposed for the government to establish a program that incentivizes the replacement of old and excessively contaminating vehicles and motorbikes with energy-efficient ones, in particular, with hybrid vehicles and motorbikes. Incentives can be in the form of duty exemptions, purchase direct subsidy, and/or purchase financing. This program has to make sure that old units are effectively discarded and not resold in the market. The purchase of hybrid vehicles and motorbikes operating partly or fully with renewable energies should be awarded with larger incentives than efficient fossil-fuel-only units.

4. Promote sustainable public transportation and reduce the number of vehicles in the Greater Male' Region

Public transportation using electric buses should be the preferred transport option in the Greater Male' Region. This requires a high quality and affordable service and disincentivizing the use of private vehicles. For the latter, it is proposed to study the feasibility of designating fossil-fuel-free areas (like in Villingili), limiting the number of plate registrations, and imposing a carbon tax on petrol and diesel use in road transport.

Liquefied Petroleum Gas Use in Cooking

1. Establish a program to replace LPG stoves with electrical induction stoves

Bottled LPG used in cooking could be entirely eliminated in Maldives if conventional LPG stoves and ovens are replaced with electric ones. In the case of stoves, modern electrical induction stoves offer the highest energy efficiency. It is proposed that the government establishes a program incentivizing the replacement of LPG stoves by modern and efficient electrical induction ones. Incentives can be in the form of duty exemptions, purchase direct subsidy, and/or purchase financing. This program has to make sure that LPG stoves are effectively discarded and not resold in the market.

6.2   Institutional Arrangements

Institutional arrangements for integrating new activities or strengthening roles within the Ministry of Environment, the Utility Regulatory Authority, and energy utilities are required to ensure successful implementation of Road Map actions. The most important aspects of this institutional arrangement are presented in Table 18 and described in the following paragraphs.

Table 18: Strengthening of Institutional Arrangements for a Successful Road Map Implementation

Ministry of Environment	Utility Regulatory Authority	Energy Utilities
• Preparation of plans and studies • Monitoring of Road Map results • Capacity building	• Verification of information submitted by utilities • Mandate to collect information from resorts and private islands • Capacity building	• Explore interconnection possibilities and synergies between energy and water • Capacity building

Source: Asian Development Bank.

Ministry of Environment

1.   Preparation of plans and studies

The Ministry of Environment should develop and keep updated the national energy balance, energy efficiency plans, and feasibility studies for the integration of innovative technologies.

- **National energy balance.** A national energy balance is necessary for the effective monitoring of Road Map results. The energy balance should be updated annually with timely reporting inputs from energy companies, island councils, main industrial players, and resorts.
- **Energy efficiency action plans.** It is recommended that specific energy efficiency action plans are developed for the Greater Male' Region; other inhabited islands; and resorts, industrial, and agricultural islands. These action plans should define energy savings targets, promote financial schemes, and propose a robust monitoring and verification mechanisms to assess energy savings.
- **Feasibility studies.** The Road Map establishes the need to implement a few pilot projects over the next years. Proper specifications for these pilot projects need to be developed by international experts under the supervision of the Ministry of Environment. The potential pilot projects are floating PV platforms, ocean energy, and fuel cells and hydrogen as energy storage.

2. Capacity building

Enabling the transition requires strengthening institutional and staff capacities in the energy sector. Capacity building of the Ministry's staff will be primarily addressed to improve knowledge on the design of effective regulation. Staff from the Ministry of Environment and the sector in general should be continuously trained, for example, on electricity pricing mechanisms and power purchase agreements. In particular, training on innovative auctioning systems as a potential option for international private sector investment will be needed.

3. Gender equality

Globally, the COVID-19 pandemic has exacerbated gender inequalities. It has also been a threat to the huge progress achieved by Maldives on gender equality and women's rights. To withstand this threat, the Ministry should reinforce the continuation of training and educational activities carried out under the POISED project. In particular, the Ministry should establish a long-term emphasis on training the female staff of the utilities in implementing the renewable energy mini-grid systems foreseen in this Road Map, and on increasing the number of female technicians and engineers. The current activities on career guidance sessions for school children for Grades 8–12 and on the promotion of women-run enterprises supplied with electricity from solar systems are crucial to achieve transformational change on gender equality.

4. Monitoring the Road Map results

Successful implementation of this Road Map requires continuous monitoring and evaluation of results. Monitoring and evaluation provide the opportunity to test planning assumptions, compare effectiveness of different approaches, adjust and correct future actions, anticipate capacity-building needs, and prepare new regulations. It also informs the national government for better delegation of responsibilities to local authorities, provides the foundation for oversight, and facilitates accountability arrangements. A mechanism led by the Ministry of Environment needs to be in place to monitor, assess, and communicate results, and coordinate actions with ministries, government offices, energy utilities, city councils, large industries (including water desalinization plants), and resorts management. A well-functioning monitoring mechanism is also useful for facilitating access to international climate finance.

Utility Regulatory Authority

1. Verification of information submitted by utilities

The future Utility Regulatory Authority should have enough capacity and adequate mechanism to verify the information submitted by utilities.

2. Mandate to collect information and enforce transparency from resorts and privately managed islands

Mandate should be conferred on the future Utility Regulatory Authority to collect information regarding generation of electricity from resorts and privately managed islands. This mandate should include adequate resources and regulation to enforce transparency in power generation operations in those islands.

3. Capacity building

Capacity building for the Utility Regulatory Authority should cover the wide range of topics the Ministry staff receives and other training areas that facilitates their verification and supervision role.

Energy Utilities

1. Exploring in detail interconnection possibilities and synergies of energy and water

Interconnection possibilities for some close-by island systems should still be studied in detail. Continuous assessments of those possibilities are needed since the demand in the islands is largely growing. Regarding the synergies of energy and water, many of the islands need to install and operate desalination plants since aquifers have been contaminated with the intrusion of saltwater or uncontrolled disposal of waste. Reverse osmosis is the most suitable technology for those plants. Reverse osmosis is an energy-intensive process that could benefit from renewable energy production. It is recommended to further explore water–energy synergies in all other inhabited islands, as well as in resorts, industrial, and agricultural islands.

2. Capacity building

Energy utilities should make all the necessary efforts to train their staff to excel in operations and maintenance of their power plants. In particular, staff from remote inhabited islands should benefit from the capacity-building programs offered by utilities.

6.3 Financing Impacts of Renewable Energy Investments

Maldives faces many difficulties in structuring the financing of its development projects, including climate change mitigation projects such as those listed in this Road Map. The main limiting factor is the reduced public sector financing capacity. This characteristic makes Maldives highly dependent on grants and soft loans from development cooperation to boost private sector investments. The foreseen actions for the base case and paradigm shift scenarios are summarized in the design and monitoring framework found in the appendixes of this report.

The base case scenario corresponds to actions and targets established by the SAP 2018–2023 and the unconditional and conditional targets established in the current Maldives' NDC for 2030.

The paradigm shift scenario goes beyond the targets established by the NDC. Pursuing this scenario may require updating of the existing NDC to establish adequate foundations for the application and negotiation of grants and loans. This is particularly important since the paradigm shift scenario requires a significant and extra effort to achieve the proposed targets. These additional efforts include:

- sustained support by multilateral development banks to specific actions and targets;
- bilateral cooperation with donor countries, which should include knowledge and technology transfer mechanisms;
- establishing alliances with foreign investors interested in the introduction of innovative renewable energy technologies; and
- strengthening knowledge sharing with other island states.

Lower generation cost from renewable energies would improve financial performance of public utilities and reduce the need for budget support to the electricity sector, thus improving the country's fiscal sustainability. Furthermore, renewable energy would positively impact the cost of electricity service as it can decrease the logistics difficulties in shipping and storing fuel across a large number of islands. Direct subsidies to electricity tariffs that could be avoided during 2020-2030 are estimated at $340 million for the base case scenario and $425 million for the paradigm shift scenario. These savings should be transformed into a financing instrument leveraging additional funds for renewable energy infrastructure, particularly for the most economically vulnerable inhabited islands. A preliminary estimate of the investments needed to achieve the targets established in this Road Map is presented in Table 19.

The base case scenario would need for the period 2020–2023 approximately $245 million in grants and loans in addition to those already approved, and an estimate of $450 million in private sector investments. For the period 2024–2030, an additional $245 million would be needed in grants and loans, and an estimate of $180 million in private sector investments.

The paradigm shift scenario would need for the period 2020–2023 approximately $315 million in grants and loans in addition to those already approved, and an estimate of $450 million in private sector investments. For the period 2024–2030, an additional $400 million would be needed in grants and loans, and an estimate of $510 million in private sector investments.

Besides the engagement of international cooperation, implementing many of the actions foreseen in both scenarios require access to domestic financing, in addition to the public sector investment programme. The national strategic framework to mobilize international climate finance to address climate change in Maldives for 2020–2024, produced by the Ministry of Environment with support from the Green Climate Fund and United Nations Environment Programme, has identified the following financing mechanisms at national level:

- Maldives Green Fund operated by the Ministry of Environment since 2019. This Fund is capitalized through the Tourist Green Tax.
- The Green Loan scheme operated by the Bank of Maldives. This scheme lends up to Rf20 million ($1.3 million at the end of 2019) to individuals and businesses looking to invest in green technology and resources.[27]
- The Renewable Energy Development Fund (RED fund), supporting utility-scale renewable energy investments.
- The Fund for Renewable Energy System Applications (FRESA Fund) operated by the Ministry of Environment and hosted by the Bank of Maldives. This is a revolving fund that focuses on small-scale private sector investment through concessional loans.

Table 19: Estimated Investments to Achieve Targets

Investment[a]	Base Case		Paradigm Shift		Financing Instrument
	Size		Size		
Period 2020–2023		($ million)		($ million)	
Interconnection - Greater Male' Region[b]	—	150	—	150	Grant/loan
Interconnection -other islands	—	15	—	20	Grant/loan
Upgrade of distribution grids	50% grids	35	50% grids	35	Grant/loan
Incentives for energy efficiency	—	20	—	40	Grant/loan
Small-scale LNG infrastructure	Reception terminal	50–100	Reception terminal	50–100	Grant/loan
Dual fuel power plant - Hulhumale'	50 MW	80–100	50 MW	80–100	Private sector - PPA
Dual fuel power plant - Thilafushi	150 MW	300–350	150 MW	300–350	Private sector - PPA
Renewable energy infrastructure - Greater Male' Region	18.5 MWp	30–35	18.5 MWp	30–35	Private sector – PPA/net metering
POISED - Other inhabited islandsb	44.5 MWp	60	44.5 MW	60	Grant/loan
Incentives for vessels replacement and solar boats	—	20	—	40	Grant/loan

continued on next page

---

[27]   Bank of Maldives. https://www.bankofmaldives.com.mv/personal-banking/personal-loans/bml-green-loan.

Table 19 *continued*

Investment[a]	Base Case Size		Paradigm Shift Size		Financing Instrument
Incentives for vehicle replacement and electric buses	—	15	—	30	Grant/loan
Incentives for LPG stoves replacement	—	15	—	25	Grant/loan
Period 2024–2030		($ million)		($ million)	
Upgrade of distribution grids	50% grids	35	50% grids	35	Grant/loan
Incentives for energy efficiency	—	40	—	80	Grant/loan
Renewable energy infrastructure – Greater Male' Region	24 MW	35–40	42.5 MW	60–70	Private sector – PPA/net metering
Renewable energy infrastructure – Other inhabited islands	61.5 MW	75–95	84 MW	100–125	Grant/loan
PV solar in resorts, agricultural, and industrial islands	50 MWp	70–80	150 MWp	200–220	Private sector
New technologies – Greater Male' Region	12 MW	20–25	70 MW	130–140	Private sector – PPA
New technologies – Other islands	18 MW	30–40	22.5 MW	40–50	Private sector – PPA
New technologies – Resort islands	16 MW	30–40	50.5 MW	80–100	Private sector
Incentives for vessels replacement and solar boats	—	40	—	80	Grant/loan
Incentives for vehicle replacement and electric buses	—	30	—	60	Grant/loan
Incentives for LPG stoves replacement	—	15	—	25	Grant/loan

LPG = liquefied petroleum gas, MW = megawatt, MWp = megawatt-peak, POISED = Preparing Outer Islands for Sustainable Energy Development, PPA = purchasing power agreement.

a   Details of investments are in the design and monitoring framework found at the appendixes of this report.

b   Grants/loans (partially or fully) approved.

Source: Asian Development Bank.

APPENDIXES

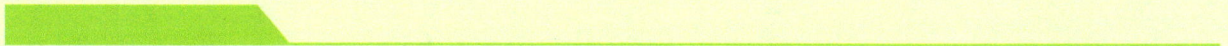

Appendix 1: Electricity Subsector, Base Case Scenario—Road Map's Design and Monitoring Framework

Impacts of the Road Map are aligned with:

Provision of sufficient, reliable, sustainable, secure, and affordable energy to all citizens

Results Chain	Performance Indicators, Targets, and Baselines	Data Sources and Reporting Mechanisms	Risks
Outcome			
1. Reliable and quality power supply and distribution is ensured to all citizens.	**By 2023:** 1a. Electricity subsidy implemented on a means-tested basis (SAP). 1b. Distribution losses in all islands kept below 7% (SAP). **By 2030:** 1c. Distribution losses in the Greater Male' Region at 5% by 2030	Reports from Maldives Energy Authority and from the future Utility Regulatory Authority. Energy utilities monthly and annual reports on distribution losses. Electricity Data Book (Ministry of Environment).	Political interference with subsidy settings. Energy distribution data are not collected properly and systematically in all islands.
2. Efficient consumption of energy without compromising the quality of life.	**By 2030:** 2a. 10% reduction of energy consumption (compared to business as usual) in all inhabited islands and in resorts, industrial, and agricultural islands.	Business–as–usual calculations presented in this Road Map. Energy utilities monthly and annual reports on energy demand in all inhabited islands.	Energy demand data are not collected properly and systematically in all islands.
3. Prominent share of renewables in the electricity sector.	**By 2023:** 3a. 24% of nationwide peak day demand supplied with renewables (20% for the Greater Male' Region and 70% for all other inhabited islands) (SAP). 3b. Provisions are made to install renewables in new public infrastructure projects (SAP). 3c. 30% of energy consumption for water and sewerage facilities across Maldives will be met with renewable energy (SAP). **By 2030:** 3d. 21% renewable energy share in electricity production: • 13% in the Greater Male' Region. • 39% in other inhabited islands. • 15% in resorts, industrial, and agricultural islands.	Energy utilities monthly and annual reports on distribution losses. Electricity Data Book (Ministry of Environment).	Electricity production and net metering data are not collected properly and systematically in all islands.

continued on next page

Results Chain	Performance Indicators, Targets, and Baselines	Data Sources and Reporting Mechanisms	Risks
4. Reduced dependence on fossil fuels for the production of electricity.	**By 2023:** 4a. Reduce fuel usage for electricity generation by 40 million liters in inhabited islands (compared to business as usual) (SAP). **By 2030:** 4b. 35% reduction of diesel usage compared to business as usual in 2030: • 26% in the Greater Male' Region. • 54% in other inhabited islands. • 26% in resorts, industrial, and agricultural islands.	Energy utilities monthly and annual reports on distribution losses. Electricity Data Book (Ministry of Environment). Reports on total imports from Maldives Customs Service.	Electricity production and net metering data are not collected properly and systematically in all islands.
Outputs			
1. Enabling regulatory environment.	**By 2023:** 1a. Regulatory Authority • Utility Regulatory Authority (URA) for integrated utility services functional by 2021 (SAP). 1b. Energy efficiency • Green energy labeling is implemented (SAP). • Provisions for green procurement in the Public Finance Act is implemented by 2022 (SAP). • Building codes are reviewed and enforced from 2022 onwards. • A buildings certification mechanism is implemented. • LED street lighting program for the Greater Male' Region and other large inhabited islands is implemented. • Inefficient lighting bulbs are phased out.	Government's appointment of Utility Regulatory Authority (URA) officers. Green energy labeling is officially implemented. Building codes revision officially accepted. Building certification mechanism officially implemented. Street lighting program officially implemented. "Zero fossil fuel energy" officially established.	Political interference with proposed measures.

continued on next page

Results Chain	Performance Indicators, Targets, and Baselines	Data Sources and Reporting Mechanisms	Risks
	1c. Implementation of a "zero fossil fuel energy" label and program for resorts islands by 2021. This program should be complemented with the implementation of mechanisms for: • mapping resorts to quantify energy efficiency potential, • energy efficiency audits, and • energy efficiency plans.		
2. Interconnection of power grids.	**By 2023:** 2a. Radial three-phase transmission grid interconnecting the Greater Male' Region. 2b. Interconnection of at least 7 small systems within the other inhabited islands.	Transmission lines commissioned.	Lack of financial resources. Delay in the works due to COVID-19 pandemic.
3. Upgrade of distribution grids and introduction of smart metering.	**By 2023:** 3a. The worst 50% of grids of inhabited islands are upgraded to meet acceptable levels of technical losses, and smart meters are introduced. **By 2030:** 3b. The remaining 50% of grids of inhabited islands are upgraded to meet acceptable level of technical losses, and smart meters are introduced in the areas served.	Grid upgrade works commissioned.	Lack of financial resources. Delay in the works due to COVID-19 pandemic.
4. Use of alternative, less polluting fuels.	**By 2023:** 4a. Dual fuel engines for the additional 50 MW power plant in Hulhumale'. 4b. Dual fuel 150 MW power plant in Thilafushi to serve the demand of the future international cargo port in Gulhifalhu.	Power plants commissioned.	Lack of financial resource or private sector interest. Delays in the construction due to slower demand growth in Hulhumale and in the construction of the future international cargo port in Gulhifalhu.

continued on next page

Results Chain	Performance Indicators, Targets, and Baselines	Data Sources and Reporting Mechanisms	Risks
5. Renewable energy infrastructure installed.	**By 2023:** 5a. At least 10 MWp of solar PV is installed under net-metering regulation (SAP). 5b. Renewable energy storage capacity is increased to 30 MWh (SAP). 5c. At least 30% of Island Waste Management Centers (IWMCs) utilize solar energy for operation (SAP). 5d. 5.0 MWp of solar PV under PPA agreement is installed over the bridge connecting Hulhule'-Male'. 5e. At least 44.5 MWp of solar PV under the Preparing Outer Islands for Sustainable Development (POISED) project in other inhabited islands. 5f. 2 x 4 MW units of waste-to-energy plant are installed in Thilafushi under a Power Purchase Agreement (PPA) agreement. **By 2030:** 5g. 24 MW of new renewable infrastructure for the Greater Male' Region: • At least additional 8 MWp of solar PV is installed in the Greater Male' Region under net-metering regulation. • 1 MWp of solar PV installed in land and over commercial roofs in Thilafushi by 2025 and 10 MWp over commercial roofs in Gulhifalhu by 2030 under PPAs. • 2 MW of wind turbine installed in Thilafushi/Gulhifalhu under PPAs. • 3 MW of rooftop micro wind turbines installed in the Greater Male' Region under net metering regulation.	Tender processes are carried out, contracts are signed, and works are commissioned.	Lack of financial resource or private sector interest. Net-metering regulation is not suitable for the projects. Unclear guidelines for the establishment of PPAs.

continued on next page

Results Chain	Performance Indicators, Targets, and Baselines	Data Sources and Reporting Mechanisms	Risks
	5h. At least 61.5 MW of new renewable energy infrastructure for the rest of the inhabited islands:		Feasibility studies are not adequately carried out.
	• At least 49.5 MWp of solar PV in upgraded POISED hybrid plants.		Lack of financial resources.
	• 2 MW in waste-to-energy plants (under PPA agreements).		Lack of interested parties.
	• 10 MW in micro rooftop wind turbines under net-metering regulation.		
	5i. At least 50 MWp of solar PV installations in resorts, industrial, and agricultural islands.		
6. Integration of technology innovation.	**By 2030:**	Tender processes are carried out, contracts are signed, and works are commissioned.	
	6a. Testing and integration of innovative renewable energy technologies (floating PV platforms, ocean energy and, hydrogen storage):		
	• 12 MW in the Greater Male' Region.		
	• 18 MW in other inhabited islands.		
	• 16 MW in resorts, industrial, and agricultural islands.		

MW = megawatt, MWh = megawatt-hour, MWp = megawatt-peak, POISED = Preparing Outer Islands for Sustainable Development, PPA = power purchase agreement, PV = photovoltaic, SAP = Strategic Action Plan, URA = Utility Regulatory Authority.
Source: Authors.

Appendix 2: Electricity Subsector, Paradigm Shift Scenario—Road Map's Design and Monitoring Framework

Impacts of the Road Map are aligned with:

Provision of sufficient, reliable, sustainable, secure, and affordable energy to all citizens

Results Chain	Performance Indicators, Targets, and Baselines	Data Sources and Reporting Mechanisms	Risks
Outcome			
1. Reliable and quality power supply and distribution is ensured to all citizens.	**By 2023:** 1a. Electricity subsidy implemented on a means-tested basis (SAP). 1b. Distribution losses in all islands kept below 7% (SAP). **By 2030:** 1c. Distribution losses in the Greater Male' Region at 5% by 2030.	Reports from Maldives Energy Authority and from the future Utility Regulatory Authority. Energy utilities monthly and annual reports on distribution losses. Electricity Data Book (Ministry of Environment).	Political interference with subsidy settings. Energy distribution data are not collected properly and systematically in all islands.
2. Efficient consumption of energy without compromising the quality of life.	**By 2030:** 2a. 20% reduction of energy consumption (compared to business as usual) in the Greater Male' Region, 15% in other inhabited islands, and 20% in resorts, industrial, and agricultural islands.	Business-as-usual calculations presented in this Road Map. Energy utilities monthly and annual reports on energy demand in all inhabited islands.	Energy demand data are not collected properly and systematically in all islands.
3. Prominent share of renewables in the electricity sector.	**By 2023:** 3a. 24% of nationwide peak day demand supplied with renewables (30% for the Greater Male' Region and 70% for all other inhabited islands) (SAP). 3b. Provisions are made to install renewables in new public infrastructure projects (SAP). 3c. 30% of energy consumption for water and sewerage facilities across Maldives will be met with renewable energy (SAP). **By 2030:** 3d. 44% renewable energy share in electricity production: • 38% in the Greater Male' Region. • 48% in other inhabited islands. • 50% in resorts, industrial, and agricultural islands.	Energy utilities monthly and annual reports on distribution losses. Electricity Data Book (Ministry of Environment).	Electricity production and net metering data are not collected properly and systematically in all islands.

continued on next page

Results Chain	Performance Indicators, Targets, and Baselines	Data Sources and Reporting Mechanisms	Risks
4. Reduced dependence on fossil fuels for the production of electricity.	**By 2023:** 4a. Reduce fuel usage for electricity generation by 70 million liters in inhabited islands (compared to business as usual) (SAP). **By 2030:** 4b. 59% reduction of diesel usage compared to business as usual in 2030: • 53% in the Greater Male' Region. • 63% in other inhabited islands. • 62% in resorts, industrial, and agricultural islands.	Energy utilities monthly and annual reports on distribution losses. Electricity Data Book (Ministry of Environment). Reports on total imports from Maldives Customs Service.	Electricity production and net metering data are not collected properly and systematically in all islands.
Outputs			
1. Enabling regulatory environment.	**By 2023:** 1a. Regulatory Authority • Utility Regulatory Authority (URA) for integrated utility services functional by 2021 (SAP). 1b. Energy efficiency: • Green energy labeling is implemented (SAP). • Provisions for green procurement in the Public Finance Act is implemented by 2022 (SAP). • Building codes are reviewed and enforced from 2022 onwards. • A building certification mechanism is implemented. • LED street lighting program for the Greater Male' Region and other large inhabited islands is implemented. • Inefficient lighting bulbs are phased out. 1c. Implementation of a "zero fossil fuel energy" label and program for resorts islands by 2021. This program should be complemented with the implementation of mechanisms for: • mapping resorts to quantify energy efficiency potential, • energy efficiency audits, and • energy efficiency plans.	Government's appointment of URA's officers. Green energy labeling is officially implemented. Building codes revision officially accepted. Building certification mechanism officially implemented. Street lighting program officially implemented. "Zero fossil fuel energy" officially established.	Political interference with proposed measures.

continued on next page

Results Chain	Performance Indicators, Targets, and Baselines	Data Sources and Reporting Mechanisms	Risks
2. Interconnection of power grids.	**By 2023:** 2a. Radial three-phase transmission grid interconnecting the 'Greater Male' Region. 2b. Interconnection of at least seven small systems within the other inhabited islands.	Transmission lines commissioned.	Lack of financial resources. Delay in the works due to COVID-19 pandemic.
3. Upgrade of distribution grids and introduction of smart metering.	**By 2023:** 3a. The worst 50% of grids of inhabited islands are upgraded to meet acceptable level of technical losses and smart meters are introduced. **By 2030:** 3b. The remaining 50% of grids of inhabited islands are upgraded to meet acceptable level of technical losses, and smart meters are introduced in the areas served.	Grid upgrade works commissioned.	Lack of financial resources. Delay in the works due to COVID-19 pandemic.
4. Use of alternative, less polluting fuels.	**By 2023:** 4a. Dual fuel engines for the additional 50 MW power plant in Hulhulmale'. 4b. Dual fuel 150 MW power plant in Thilafushi to serve the demand of the future international cargo port in Gulhifalhu.	Power plants commissioned.	Lack of financial resources or private sector interest. Delays in the construction due to slower demand growth in Hulhumale and in the construction of the future international cargo port in Gulhifalhu.
5. Renewable energy infrastructure installed.	**By 2023:** 5a. At least 10 MWp of solar PV is installed under net-metering regulation (SAP). 5b. Renewable energy storage capacity is increased to 30 MWh (SAP). 5c. At least 30% of Island Waste Management Centers (IWMCs) utilize solar energy for operation (SAP). 5d. 5.0 MWp of solar PV under PPA agreement is installed over the bridge connecting Hulhule'-Male'. 5e. At least 44.5 MWp of solar PV under POISED are in other inhabited islands. 5f. 2x4 MW units of waste-to-energy plant are installed in Thilafushi under a PPA agreement.	Tender processes are carried out, contracts are signed, and works are commissioned.	Lack of financial resources or private sector interest. Net-metering regulation is not suitable for the projects. Unclear guidelines for the establishment of PPAs.

continued on next page

Results Chain	Performance Indicators, Targets, and Baselines	Data Sources and Reporting Mechanisms	Risks
	By 2030:		
	5g. 42.5 MW of new renewable energy infrastructure for the Greater Male' Region:		
	• At least additional 9.5 MWp of solar PV is installed in the Greater Male' Region under net-metering regulation.		
	• 5 MWp of solar PV installed in land and over commercial roofs in Thilafushi by 2025 and 18 MWp over commercial roofs in Gulhifalhu by 2030 under PPAs.		
	• 2MW of wind turbine installed in Thilafushi/ Gulhifalhu under a PPA.		
	• 8 MW of rooftop micro wind turbines installed in the Greater Male' Region under net-metering regulation.		
	5h. At least 84 MW of new renewable energy infrastructure for the rest of inhabited islands:		
	• At least 67 MWp of solar PV in upgraded POISED hybrid plants.		
	• 2 MW in waste-to-energy plants (under PPA agreements).		
	• 15 MW in micro rooftop wind turbines under net-metering regulation.		
	5i. At least 150 MWp of solar PV installations in resorts, industrial, and agricultural islands.		
6. Integration of technology innovation.	**By 2030:**	Tender processes are carried out, contracts are signed, and works are commissioned.	Feasibility studies are not adequately carried out. Lack of financial resources. Lack of interested parties.
	6a. Testing and integration of innovative renewable energy technologies (floating PV platforms, ocean energy, and hydrogen storage):		
	• 70 MW in the Greater Male' Region.		
	• 22.5 MW in other inhabited islands.		
	• 50 MW in resorts, industrial, and agricultural islands.		

MW = megawatt, MWh = megawatt-hour, MWp = megawatt-peak, POISED = Preparing Outer Islands for Sustainable Development, PPA = power purchase agreement, PV = photovoltaic, SAP = Strategic Action Plan, URA = Utility Regulatory Authority.

Source: Authors.

Appendix 3: Transport and Cooking Subsectors, Base Case Scenario—Road Map's Design and Monitoring Framework

Impacts of the Road Map are aligned with:

Provision of sufficient, reliable, sustainable, secure, and affordable energy to all citizens

Results Chain	Performance Indicators, Targets, and Baselines	Data Sources and Reporting Mechanisms	Risks
Outcome			
1. Strengthened maritime infrastructure and services to enhance socioeconomic growth.	**By 2023:** 1a. An efficient public ferry service is operational in all administrative islands (SAP).	Reports from Maldives Transport Authority.	Prolonged economic crisis preventing needed investments.
2. Increased concerted efforts to reduce congestion and ease accessibility to roads in the Greater Male' Region.	**By 2023:** 2a. Vehicle congestion is reduced by 30% compared to 2018 levels. 2b. At least 60% of the population utilize regularly sustainable public transportation.	Reports from Maldives Transport Authority.	Number of vehicles increases over targets. Public transportation does not evolve into the aimed high quality and comfort.
3. Reduced dependence on fossil fuels in sea transport.	**By 2030:** 3a. 22% of fuel use reduction in sea transport.	Reports from Maldives Transport Authority. Reports on total imports from Maldives Customs Service.	Prolonged economic crisis preventing needed investments.
4. Reduced dependence on fossil fuels in road transport.	**By 2030:** 4a. 22% of fuel use reduction in road transport.	Reports from Maldives Transport Authority. Reports on total imports from Maldives Customs Service.	Prolonged economic crisis preventing needed investments.
5. Reduced dependence on fossil fuels used in cooking.	**By 2030:** 5a. 35% of Liquefied Petroleum Gas (LPG) use reduction in cooking.	Reports on total imports from Maldives Customs Service.	Prolonged economic crisis preventing needed investments.

continued on next page

Results Chain	Performance Indicators, Targets, and Baselines	Data Sources and Reporting Mechanisms	Risks
Outputs			
1. Replacement of inefficient vessels.	**By 2030:** 1a. Replacement of a number of inefficient vessels with the help of a dedicated government program providing economic incentives for such replacement. The number of units replaced shall be calculated by the respective authority with the overall aim of reducing by 20% the average specific consumption of vessels in Maldives.	Reports from Maldives Transport Authority.	Lack of financial resources to implement measure.
2. Introduction of hybrid solar boats.	**By 2030:** 2a. Promote the introduction of solar boats until a 2.5% share is achieved.	Reports from Maldives Transport Authority.	Lack of financial resources to implement measure.
3. Natural gas as alternative fuel for large vessels.	**By 2023:** 3a. Feasibility study to assess benefits and costs of fueling ships running on liquefied natural gas (LNG) and docking at the future cargo port in Gulhifalhu.	Feasibility study report.	Lack of financial resources to implement measure.
4. Hydrogen as alternative fuel for jetties.	**By 2023:** 4a. Feasibility study to assess benefits and costs of promoting jetties transformation into hydrogen–fueled jetties using small fueling stations located on the islands that store hydrogen produced with their excess renewable energy. **By 2030:** 4b. If the feasibility study is successful, a pilot project will be established to test hydrogen–fueled jetties.	Feasibility study report. Pilot project is commissioned.	Lack of financial resources or private sector interest.
5. Replacement of inefficient vehicles and motorbikes	**By 2030:** 1a. Replacement of a number of inefficient vehicles and motorbikes with the help of a dedicated government program providing economic incentives for such replacement. The number of units replaced shall be calculated by the respective authority with the overall aim of reducing by 20% the average specific consumption of road vehicles in Maldives.	Reports from Maldives Transport Authority.	Lack of financial resources to implement measure.

continued on next page

Results Chain	Performance Indicators, Targets, and Baselines	Data Sources and Reporting Mechanisms	Risks
6. Introduction of electric buses, vehicles, and motorbikes.	**By 2030:** 6a. Promote the introduction of full electric buses, vehicles, and motorbikes nationwide until at least 2.5% share is achieved.	Reports from Maldives Transport Authority.	Lack of financial resources to implement measure.
7. Reduction of vehicles registration	**By 2023:** 7a. Establishment of a maximum annual number of new plates for the largest cities in Maldives.	Reports from Maldives Transport Authority.	Political interference with this measure.
8. Natural gas as alternative fuel for large vessels.	**By 2023:** 8a. Feasibility study to assess benefits and costs of introducing gas-fueled vehicles and fueling stations in the Greater Male' Region in case the installation of a small-scale LNG infrastructure is decided for.	Feasibility study report.	Lack of financial resources to implement this measure.
9. Replacement of LPG stoves by electric induction stoves.	**By 2030:** 9a. Awareness campaign and promotion of microcredit program aiming at the replacement of 35% of LPG stoves with electric induction stoves and reducing or removing subsidies to LPG used in cooking.	Reports on total imports from Maldives Customs Service.	Prolonged economic crisis preventing needed investments.

LNG = liquefied natural gas, LPG = liquefied petroleum gas.
Source: Authors.

Appendix 4: Transport and Cooking Subsectors, Paradigm Shift Scenario—Road Map's Design and Monitoring Framework

Impacts of the Road Map are aligned with:

Provision of sufficient, reliable, sustainable, secure, and affordable energy to all citizens

Results Chain	Performance Indicators, Targets, and Baselines	Data Sources and Reporting Mechanisms	Risks
Outcome			
1. Strengthened maritime infrastructure and services to enhance socioeconomic growth.	**By 2023:** 1a. An efficient public ferry service is operational in all administrative islands (SAP).	Reports from Maldives Transport Authority.	Prolonged economic crisis preventing needed investments.
2. Increased concerted efforts to reduce congestion and ease accessibility to roads in the Greater Male' Region	**By 2023:** 2a. Vehicle congestion is reduced by 30% compared to 2018 levels. 2b. At least 60% of the population utilize regularly sustainable public transportation.	Reports from Maldives Transport Authority.	Number of vehicles increases over targets. Public transportation does not evolve into the aimed high quality and comfort.
3. Reduced dependence on fossil fuels in sea transport.	**By 2030:** 3a. 42% of fuel use reduction in sea transport.	Reports from Maldives Transport Authority. Reports on total imports from Maldives Customs Service.	Prolonged economic crisis preventing needed investments.
4. Reduced dependence on fossil fuels in road transport.	**By 2030:** 4a. 52% of fuel use reduction in road transport.	Reports from Maldives Transport Authority. Reports on total imports from Maldives Customs Service.	Prolonged economic crisis preventing needed investments.
5. Reduced dependence on fossil fuels used in cooking.	**By 2030:** 5a. 50% of LPG use reduction in cooking.	Reports on total imports from Maldives Customs Service.	Prolonged economic crisis preventing needed investments.

continued on next page

Results Chain	Performance Indicators, Targets, and Baselines	Data Sources and Reporting Mechanisms	Risks
Outputs			
1. Replacement of inefficient vessels.	**By 2030:** 1a. Replacement of a number of inefficient vessels with the help of a dedicated government program providing economic incentives for such replacement. The number of units replaced shall be calculated by the respective authority with the overall aim of reducing by 40% the average specific consumption of vessels in Maldives.	Reports from Maldives Transport Authority.	Lack of financial resources to implement measure.
2. Introduction of hybrid solar boats.	**By 2030:** 2a. Promote the introduction of solar boats until a 2.5% share is achieved.	Reports from Maldives Transport Authority.	Lack of financial resources to implement measure.
3. Natural gas as alternative fuel for large vessels.	**By 2023:** 3a. Feasibility study to assess benefits and costs of fueling ships running on LNG and docking at the future cargo port in Gulhifalhu.	Feasibility study report.	Lack of financial resources to implement measure.
4. Hydrogen as alternative fuel for jetties.	**By 2023:** 4a. Feasibility study to assess benefits and costs of promoting jetties transformation into hydrogen-fueled jetties using small fueling stations located on the islands that store hydrogen produced with their excess renewable energy. **By 2030:** 4b. If the feasibility study is successful, a pilot project will be established to test hydrogen-fueled jetties.	Feasibility study report. Pilot project is commissioned.	Lack of financial resources or private sector interest.
5. Replacement of inefficient vehicles and motorbikes	**By 2030:** 5a. Replacement of a number of inefficient vehicles and motorbikes with the help of a dedicated government program providing economic incentives for such replacement. The number of units replaced shall be calculated by the respective authority with the overall aim of reducing by 40% the average specific consumption of road vehicles in Maldives.	Reports from Maldives Transport Authority.	Lack of financial resources to implement measure.

continued on next page

Appendix 4 continued

Results Chain	Performance Indicators, Targets, and Baselines	Data Sources and Reporting Mechanisms	Risks
6. Introduction of electric buses, vehicles, and motorbikes.	**By 2030:** 6a. Promote the introduction of full electric buses, vehicles, and motorbikes nationwide until a 20% share is achieved.	Reports from Maldives Transport Authority.	Lack of financial resources to implement measure.
7. Reduction of vehicles registration	**By 2023:** 7a. Establishment of a maximum annual number of new plates for the largest cities in Maldives.	Reports from Maldives Transport Authority.	Political interference with this measure.
8. Natural gas as alternative fuel for large vessels.	**By 2023:** 8a. Feasibility study to assess benefits and costs of introducing gas-fueled vehicles and fueling stations in the Greater Male' Region in case the installation of a small-scale LNG infrastructure is decided for.	Feasibility study report.	Lack of financial resources to implement this measure.
9. Replacement of LPG stoves by electric induction stoves.	**By 2030:** 9a. Awareness campaign and promotion of microcredit program aiming at the replacement of 50% of LPG stoves with electric induction stoves and reducing or removing subsidies to LPG used in cooking.	Reports on total imports from Maldives Customs Service.	Prolonged economic crisis preventing needed investments.

LNG = liquefied natural gas, LPG = liquefied petroleum gas.
Source: Authors.

REFERENCES

ADB. 2014. *Towards a Carbon-Neutral Energy Sector: Maldives Energy Roadmap, 2014–2020*. Manila.

ADB. 2018. *Asian Development Outlook: Sustaining Development through Public-Private Partnership*. Manila.

ADB. 2019. *Maldives Economic Update 2019*. Manila.

BeCitizen. 2010. *Maldives 2009 Carbon Audit Report*. Paris.

Centre for Understanding Sustainable Practice (CUSP), Robert Gordon University. 2011. *Marine Energy in Maldives: Pre-Feasibility Report on Scottish Support for Maldives Marine Energy Implementation*. Aberdeen.

Climate Investment Fund. 2019. Preparing Outer Island Sustainable Electricity Development Project (POISED). *CIF-GDI Delivery Challenge Case Study*.

P. Contestabile et al. 2017. Offshore Wind and Wave Energy Assessment around Malè and Magoodhoo Island (Maldives). *Sustainability*. 9(4):613. DOI: 10.3390/su9040613, Basel.

Government of Maldives. 2019. *Strategic Action Plan for the Period 2018–2023*. Male'.

Government of Maldives, Ministry of Environment and Energy. 2010. *Maldives National Energy Policy and Strategy*. Male'.

Government of Maldives, Ministry of Environment and Energy. 2015a. *Greater Male' Region Renewable Energy Integration Plan*. Male'.

Government of Maldives, Ministry of Environment and Energy. 2015b. *National Biodiversity Strategy and Action Plan of Maldives, 2016–2025*. Male'.

Government of Maldives, Ministry of Environment and Energy. 2016a. *Maldives Energy Policy and Strategy 2016*. Male'.

Government of Maldives, Ministry of Environment and Energy. 2016b. *Second National Communication of Maldives to the United Nations Framework Convention on Climate Change*. Male'.

Government of Maldives, Ministry of Environment and Energy. 2016c. *State of the Environment Report*. Male'.

Government of Maldives, Ministry of Environment and Energy. 2017. *Solar Resource Renewable Energy Roadmap for the Republic of Maldives*. Male'.

Government of Maldives, Ministry of Environment and Energy. 2018. *Electricity Data Book 2018*. Male'.

Government of Maldives, Ministry of Environment. 2020. *National Strategic Framework to Mobilize International Climate Finance to Address Climate Change in Maldives, 2020–2024*. Male'.

Government of Maldives, Ministry of Health. 2019. *Maldives Demographic and Health Survey*. Male'.

Government of Maldives, Ministry of National Planning and Infrastructure, National Bureau of Statistics. 2020. *Statistical Yearbook of Maldives 2020*. Male'.

L. Guppy et al. 2018. Groundwater and Sustainable Development Goals: Analysis of Interlinkages. *UNU-INWEH Report Series*. Issue 04. Hamilton, Canada: United Nations University Institute for Water, Environment and Health.

Hydrogen Council. 2020. *Path to Hydrogen Competitiveness: A Cost Perspective*. Brussels.

ICF International Inc. 2018. *LNG Study for Power Generation in Male'*. New Delhi.

IRENA. 2015. *Renewable Energy Roadmap for the Republic of Maldives*. Abu Dhabi.

Maldives Customs Service. 2019. *Total Imports 2019*. https://www.customs.gov.mv/Media/Documents/downloads. Male'.

K. Nam. 2019. *Financing the 2030 Energy Transition: ADB's Approach in Supporting Low Carbon Development*. Presentation at Asian Development Bank. Bangkok. 19 March.

M. Purcell and T. Gilbert. 2015. *Wind Resource Mapping in Maldives: Mesoscale Wind Modeling Report*. Washington, DC: World Bank Group.

Scaling-Up Renewable Energy Programme. 2012. *Investment Plan—Maldives*. Male'.

US National Renewable Energy Laboratory. 2003. *Wind Energy Resource Atlas of Sri Lanka and Maldives*. Golden.

World Bank. 2020a. *Project Appraisal Document of the Accelerating Sustainable Private Investments in Renewable Energy (ASPIRE) Project*. Report No. 145392-MV. Washington, DC.

World Bank. 2020b. *Maldives Development Update: In Stormy Seas*. Washington, DC.